BAHAMAS
Out Island Odyssey

For detailed travel information on the Bahama Out Islands, contact:

Bahama Out Island Promotion Board
1100 Lee Wagener Boulevard, Suite 206
Ft. Lauderdale, Florida 33315
Tel: 800-OUT ISLANDS (800-688-4752, 305-359-8099)
Fax: 305-359-8098

BAHAMAS
Out Island Odyssey

by Nan Jeffrey

family • adventure • travel

distributed to the book trade by
Menasha Ridge Press

Avalon House Publishing

Editor   Tim Coggeshall
Book Design   Avalon House Publishing

Printed in the United States Of America
10 9 8 7 6 5 4 3 2 1

Jeffrey, Nan, 1949—
        Bahamas: out island odyssey
            /Nan Jeffrey
            p. cm.
        ISBN 0-9627562-3-7 (pbk.)
        1. Travel
        F1651.J44 1995
        917.296—dc20   LC 94-73997

distributed by: **marine orders & editorial requests:**
Menasha Ridge Press   Avalon House, c/o HFCO
3169 Cahaba Heights Rd.   P.O. Box 126
Birmingham, AL 35243 USA   Ashland, MA 01721 USA
Orders: 1-800-247-9437   Tel: 1-508-881-4602
                                        Fax: 1-508-881-3846

Contents

Acknowledgments

I would like to thank all those who made this book possible. I extend a special thanks to the Bahama Out Island Promotion Board, Island Express Airlines, Stella Maris Resort, Coconut Cove Hotel, Two Turtles Inn, Hotel Greenwood Inn, Unique Village, The Cove Eleuthera, Tom Jones, Valentine's Yacht Club & Inn, Hope Town Hideaways, Hope Town Harbour Lodge, Schooner's Landing, Pelican Beach Villas, Guana Beach Resort, Bluff House and Green Turtle Club. I would also like to thank Tim Coggeshall for his editorial assistance and the many wonderful Bahamian people we met during our Out Island Odyssey.

Author's Note

In writing this book, my purpose was to inspire others to discover the many joys of a trip to the Bahama Out Islands. The young and the old, families with children and couples on their own, those with a sense of adventure and those who favor the tried and true—all can enjoy and benefit from a visit to this nation of islands.

Bahamas—Out Island Odyssey is neither a guide book nor a travelogue, but rather a taste of Out Island life as seen and experienced from the vantage point of a visitor. We hope this book serves as an entertaining, enlightening read for armchair travelers. If, after reading it, you feel an overwhelming urge to ramble through the islands or go find your own private hideaway, so much the better. For us, the Bahama Out Islands will always remain a favorite destination.

The Out Islands

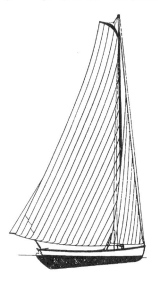

Mention the word "Bahamas" to most people and they immediately visualize all sorts of delightful images: sunshine and warmth, palm trees and tropical waters, coral reefs and abundant sea life—a beach lover's, sun-worshiper's, snorkeler's paradise. Their expression invariably takes on a dreamy look of longing and regret and envy, as though the Bahamas represents some desirable, yet wholly unattainable fantasy. Little do they realize that the Bahamas, unlike many other tropical destinations, are not just the territory of the very rich, the very leisured, or the newlywed. They are, in fact, one of the prime destinations for anyone with a yen for an escape from winter cold or summer heat, for a deserted beach or simply a slower pace. The Out Islands in particular possess a physical beauty, charm and a social tempo that bears little resemblance to the frenzied activity of Nassau or Freeport. Varied and equally inviting, they offer the kind of respite one yearns for in this frenetic age.

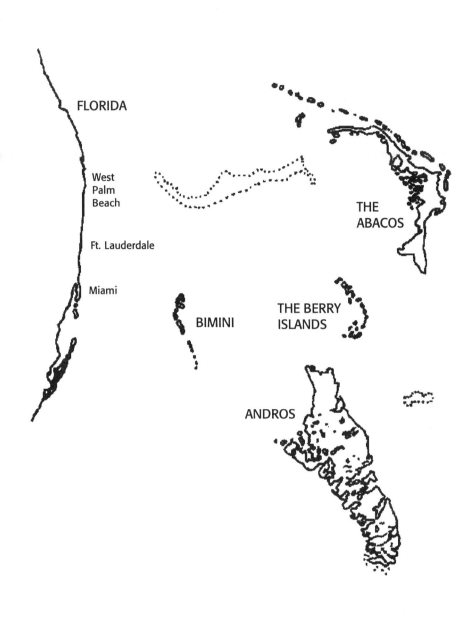

FLORIDA

West
Palm
Beach

Ft. Lauderdale

Miami

THE
ABACOS

BIMINI

THE BERRY
ISLANDS

ANDROS

The Out Islands
Of The Bahamas

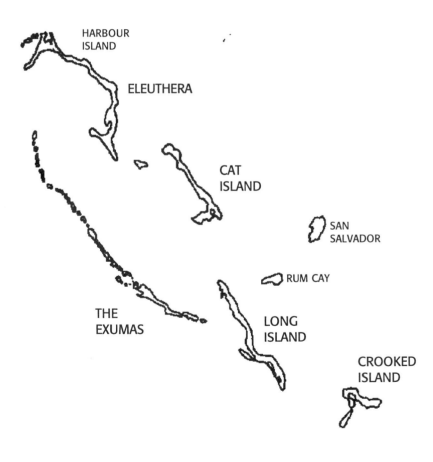

HARBOUR
ISLAND

ELEUTHERA

CAT
ISLAND

SAN
SALVADOR

RUM CAY

THE
EXUMAS

LONG
ISLAND

CROOKED
ISLAND

Despite their enthusiastic response, many people have only a vague idea where the Bahamas actually are. When not confusing it with Bermuda, they place it somewhere in the Caribbean. The Bahamas actually lie in places as close as fifty miles off the coast of Florida, while extending almost as far south as Cuba. They also often mistake Nassau for the entire Bahamas, a misconception tantamount to equating New York City with the United States. The Bahamas comprise about seven hundred islands extending over five hundred miles, a fact that can amaze even those who have been there. One acquaintance, veteran of two cruises to Nassau, greeted this piece of information with an incredulous "I didn't know there were any other islands!" One of the more intriguing cases of mistaken identity involved the U.S. Postal Service which, when forwarding a letter from our young niece to our sons in the Bahamas, sent the letter to Barbados instead.

Nor do their geographic vagaries cease upon arrival in the country itself. While Nassau seems to conjure up a clear sense of origin, the Out Islands create a daunting confusion in many visitors' minds. One young couple, contentedly riding an island ferry in the Abacos, was overheard asking what that island over there was. It happened to be the island they had just left.

Sailors usually suffer none of the geographic confusion of their land-based counterparts. Why? They know that the Out Islands represent one of the best cruising grounds in the world, a treasure-trove of good sailing breezes, endless gunkholing, secluded anchorages, private beaches, excellent fishing, and a laidback sailing fraternity. Curving like a protective arm, the Out Islands form the outer edge of land and shoal waters in the Bahama chain. Protected themselves from Atlantic seas by barrier reefs, they offer excellent swimming and quiet waters, ideal for all ages. These islands possess a subtler beauty than the lush, mountainous spectacle of many Caribbean islands. Low and narrow, they seem in places mere wisps of land, their tall coconut palms and casuarina pines often the highest visible point. White and pink sand beaches line much of the island shores, while coral reefs support an almost unparalleled underwater sea life.

The Bahamas straddles two worlds, from the simple living conditions and slow pace in the south to the more modern and commercial islands in the north. None of the Out Islands, however, exhibit a high degree of organization, possessing instead a charm that far outshines any pronounced efficiency. It is a country of contrasts and contradictions that somehow maintain a friendly coexistence: the crowded urban streets of Nassau and the lazy tempo of the sparsely populated Out Islands; the small, elegant resorts and accompanying straggle of primitive kerosene-lit homes; the impeccable service of a hotel staff and the hopeless confusion of a mailboat delivery. The Blacks and Whites who inhabit the islands with no noticeable racial tension pride themselves on their philosophy of acceptance, with the frequently heard "no problem" practically a national motto. Each inhabited island has its own distinct character, from its physical attributes to the type of people, towns, industry and activities one finds there. All, however, possess that intangible magic that distinguishes the Bahamas from other tropical islands.

It is perhaps the close proximity to Florida that finally renders the Bahamas so thoroughly magical. Separated by the Gulf Stream, the two places are the antithesis of each other, the one overpopulated, overdeveloped and over-touristed, the other a place of unspoiled nature, few inhabitants, and a comparative handful of tourists. Anyone sharing a strip of sand in Florida with a few thousand other people would find it hard to imagine that a mere one hundred or so miles away lies what is perhaps the beach paradise of the world, a place where sharing a beach with more than a dozen other people is practically undignified.

The Bahama Out Islands are equally appealing to those seeking a relaxing respite from the daily grind to those with a zest for adventure. A destination with little in the way of expansive resorts or amusement centers, mass tourist development or commercialism, the Out Islands seem refreshingly authentic, a place that exists for itself rather than to satisfy some tourist fantasy. In so doing, it has retained a cultural integrity in the face of growing tourism. Above all, it is a place for those who seek nothing more than the quiet, creative pleasures of a patch of sand or dirt path, a sleepy village or coral reef, a brilliant sunset or soft sea breeze. The Out Islands are what their name implies: far from the teaming life-style of the modern day. They are a journey well worth taking.

* * * *

Cat Island, The Exumas & Long Island

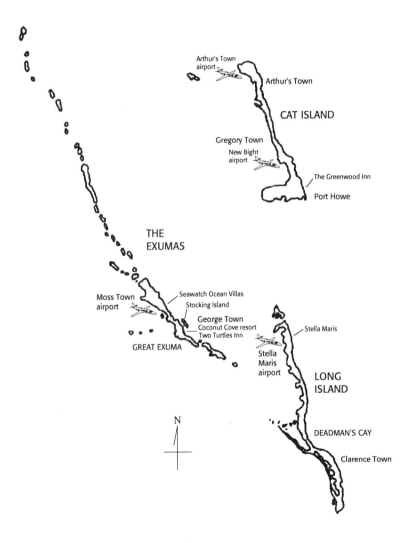

Arthur's Town
airport

Arthur's Town

CAT ISLAND

Gregory Town
New Bight
airport

The Greenwood Inn

Port Howe

THE
EXUMAS

Moss Town
airport

Seawatch Ocean Villas
Stocking Island

George Town
Coconut Cove resort
Two Turtles Inn

GREAT EXUMA

Stella Maris

Stella
Maris
airport

LONG
ISLAND

N

DEADMAN'S CAY

Clarence Town

Eleuthera, Harbour Island,
New Providence & Spanish Wells

The Abacos & Grand Bahama

GRAND
BAHAMA

West End

Freeport

Cooper's Town

GREEN TURTLE CAY
New Plymouth
Bluff House
Green Turtle Club

Treasure Cay

GREAT GUANA CAY
Guana Beach Resort & Marina

MAN-O-WAR CAY
Schooner's Landing

ELBOW CAY
Hope Town
Hope Town Hideaways
Hope Town Harbour Lodge

Marsh Harbour
Pelican Beach Villas

THE
ABACOS

N

Cherokee Sound

GREAT ABACO

Long Island

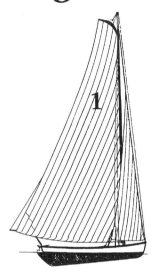

$\mathbf{S}$leepy, somnolent, peaceful, this is a place for those who enjoy quiet and solitude, natural surroundings, gentle rolling land, hot, still beaches, and a feeling that humans are a rarity. Long Island provides a taste of the Third World, where self-sufficiency, simplicity and doing without determine the pace of life.

The Arrival

When we contemplated a trip to the Bahamas in late February, we decided to begin our Out Island travels in the south. Starting with Long Island, the southernmost island with any recognizable tourist facilities (other than Great Inagua), we planned to follow the warm weather as it moved north with the coming of spring.

Having set the stage for our departure by visiting the Ft. Lauderdale beach, we packed for the flight. The final tally was an eclectic mix encompassing such diverse items as snorkel and fins, a lap-top computer and thirty cloth diapers. As always when traveling, our goal was to take only as much gear as we could carry in one load, in this case three frame packs, one baby backpack (with the baby in it), two violins, one briefcase, and one handbag. Unless you are traveling to the Bahamas on a cruise ship to Nassau or on your own yacht, flying is the only way to get there. Having sailed twice, a trip involving adverse prevailing winds, the temperamental Gulf Stream, precision timing, and various navigational hazards, I would have considered that the most adventurous mode of travel. But that was before I went by small plane. Admittedly, flying has never been my strong point. While Third World destinations, exotic cultures, shaky governments and dubious health conditions have never deterred me, flying has always sent the heart racing and the blood pounding. My sympathies are entirely with those who clutch the armrests during take-off, say a small prayer before each landing, and don't ease up much in between. My ears are primed throughout to pick up any slight variance in engine noise, while air turbulence practically puts me in a coma. Undoubtedly, it is the sense of not being in control, of being at the mercy of some unseen pilot that renders so many people a basket of nerves at the mere thought of air travel. In my case, the one exception is the jumbo jet, a contraption so large that I can almost pretend I've never really left the ground.

Milling around the Ft. Lauderdale airport with only a handful of fellow passengers, I began to suspect the worst. Finally, unable to quell my curiosity, I asked the airline attendant how large the plane was. "A Cessna ten-seater," she replied, "including the pilot." Little did I know that this was the largest airplane we would travel in over the next two months.

Once on board, Tristan and Colin, our fourteen-year-old sons, were seated right behind the pilot; Kevin, two large men, and their equally-endowed wives were in the middle; and Gwyneth and I were in the back. As with all small planes, the loading ritual was directed by the pilot, a process that set you wondering just how critical a few misplaced pounds really were.

At the first revving of the twin engines, Gwyneth Islay, our seven-month-old daughter, latched onto my breast like a drowning man to a lifering. Her nursing merged into blissful sleep, a welcome state of affairs, until we encountered our first in a series of thunderheads just east of the Berry Islands. I had just finished admiring the cluster of small islands strewn across the turquoise waters below, even picking out the very one where we'd anchored for my birthday ten years ago, when I noticed the billowing clouds ahead. Waiting for the pilot to take evasive action, I watched in disbelief as he ignored the whole mess, plunging the plane in with what I regarded as gross negligence. Within seconds the plane was bouncing around like some nauseating thrill ride at a county fair. Gwyneth sent up a howl that was fortunately drowned out by the engines. Clinging to the hand strap, and making a valiant effort to keep the baby from bouncing off the ceiling, I glared forward at the pilot. What was he doing in my moment of need? Giving the clouds a casual glance, he switched the whole plane on autopilot, turned around, and proceeded to give the boys pointers on chart navigation. For the first time it occurred to me that seeing the pilot in action might not provide the solace I'd expected.

Our first stop was North Eleuthera, an airport only recognizable by its small landing strip. Passing through customs involved little more than a token handful of questions, a cursory glance at our luggage, and a quick

Stella Maris Resort, Long Island

Reservations: 800-426-0466, 305-359-8236
Direct Phone: 809-336-2106
Fax (US office): 305-359-8238

Accommodations: 120-person capacity in a variety of accommodations, including hotel rooms, apartment cottages, ocean villas, and private homes.

Getting There: Take a commercial flight from Ft. Lauderdale or Nassau to Long Island (Stella Maris' private plane will also pick up in Ft. Lauderdale, Nassau, or Exuma upon request); take a short taxi ride from the airport to the resort.

Local Transport: Resort vehicles and bicycles, and taxis.

Meals: Either MAP, EP or by the meal in the main dining room.

Amenities: 3 pools, table tennis, ocean- and Caribbean-side beaches, terraces and dining areas, free bicycles, small sail boats, day outings to beaches (Deal's Beach and Cape Santa Maria), tennis courts ($15/hour), boutique, protected marina with boat excursions for resort guests, laundry service.

Phones: Available only at the front desk.

Electricity: Long Island has utility electricity, but for now the resort generates its own power.

Water: Ample running water in the rooms; drinking water is taken as needed from the fountain by the hotel lobby.

Laundry: The hotel has a laundry service (rates are by the piece).

Nearby Food Stores: The Stella Maris general store, the Simms and Burnt Ground Village food stores; and the Hilltop Bakery.

Highlights:

• Families are especially welcome, with the relaxed atmosphere, congenial dining, and accommodations well suited to children of all ages.

• The resort blends in well with the environment and never seems to be crowded.

• There are lots of good walks and bike rides and great beaches within easy reach.

• A variety of pool and beach areas, an outdoor ping-pong table (with night lighting-great for teenagers).

• Complimentary bicycles in good condition.

• Daily planned activities (often at no cost) including excursions to nearby beaches, boat trips (for fishing, diving, snorkeling, or sightseeing), and a weekly barbecue party in "the cave" (for all ages).

• Accommodations and food are excellent, and the staff friendly, organized and attentive.

• Somewhat isolated at the northern tip of Long Island, this is a place for those who enjoy nature, good service and getting away from it all.

• The setting is spectacular, overlooking the Atlantic shore, although beach swimming is best done elsewhere.

nip into the most unglamorous of bathrooms. Our fellow passengers having departed, we now had the whole plane to ourselves for the final flight to Long Island. No clouds were in evidence to the south, a state of affairs that rendered me positively giddy with relief. Tristan and Colin, their ears in a perpetual state of ringing, sought seats farther back, while Kevin jumped into the co-pilot's seat. Gwyneth, now wide awake and her usual active, inquisitive self, began to prowl the aircraft in an alarming fashion. By the end of the trip, sunglasses, keys, purse and mutilated magazines all bore evidence of her progress.

The flight followed the southwestern line of Eleuthera and Cat Island before landing at the tiny Stella Maris airstrip in northern Long Island. We found one short runway, a small, deserted building, a handful of parked private planes, and no one in sight. Heat bore down on us, the air smelled delicious and fresh, leaves rustled gently in the trees, and a sense of timelessness prevailed, as though the passing hours were a figment of the imagination. Even the arrival and departure of the plane seemed unreal, with us the only evidence that it had really happened. Standing there surrounded by luggage without a sound to be heard, we felt like the miles traveled had been far more than a short plane ride. Florida must have existed in another lifetime.

Stella Maris, our resort destination, was a mile and a half up the dirt road, a distance that made us glad we could carry everything at one go. Taxis are available and undoubtedly what the ordinary traveler uses, but like many of the services in the Bahamas, at times the cost can outweigh the convenience for budget travelers like ourselves. We walked.

In a way, walking made the whole experience more mysterious. Approaching on foot, you hardly know that

Stella Maris exists, its entrance simply a dirt road leading to a low, attractive building surrounded by lush tropical vegetation. Checking in at the front desk, we were whisked the short distance to our villa in a van, feeling slightly absurd after hoofing it all the way from the airport. The villa was wonderful: two rooms with overhead fans, a large terrace with table and chairs, attractive bathroom, dining table, and (best of all) a refrigerator. There was even a crib set up in the bedroom. The only drawback was the tile floors, common fare in the Bahamas, but doom to a baby with a compulsion for standing up and toddling about on wobbly legs. All elegance was banished as rugs, pillows and spare blankets were heaped on the floor around her. Surveying the carnage, Kevin remarked, "It takes four people to mind one baby?"

We loved Stella Maris on sight. Across from the villa, a grove of graceful trees, an expanse of grass and flowering shrubs gave way to the white roof of the pool, glimpses of blue water, and the endless, clear sky. We could hear waves washing the beach below. A dirt path crested the hill beyond our villa, disappearing into a mass of low island growth dotted with delicate wild flowers. No human sounds penetrated the aura of peaceful isolation. No cars or airplanes. No lawn movers or weedwhackers. No motorboats or jet-skis. It seemed like stepping off onto another planet, into another day and age, another lifetime altogether. Even Stella Maris itself seemed a fantasy, something that existed in name only. Its scattered buildings and narrow roads, its three pools, extensive staff and other guests were practically invisible, lost in a maze of palm trees and flowering hibiscus, whispering pines and the sounds of the sea. The word "resort" seemed a misnomer, with its implied elements of pampered luxury and grandiose entertainment. Here, the overwhelming sense was one of having arrived, not at some resort or vacation spot, but at an island. Remote, quiet, peaceful, it offered an ideal introduction to the Out Islands.

* * * *

Winter Olympics

Venturing forth from the villa, Tristan and Colin discovered an outdoor pingpong table (complete with floodlights), the three swimming pools, an assortment of courtesy bicycles, and a recreation room, this last equipped with the one and only television at the resort. Eager to watch the last of the Winter Olympic coverage, we converged that evening with a host of other sports enthusiasts, only to discover that television on Long Island had some interesting quirks, principally a habit of turning into a mass of static every time the telephone was used. As calls invariably occurred during the sports events, only to cease just as the ads came on, a certain note of hilarity soon crept into the proceedings, with all of us speculating as to what we were missing. Olympic diehards to the end, eager to see the outcome of the women's figure skating, Tristan and Colin persevered as other guests wandered off to bed. Finally, a bleary-eyed maintenance worker poked his head in the door, spotted the two boys, and gave up the wait.

"Turn out the lights and lock up when you leave," was his parting remark.

In retrospect, they weren't sure which was the bigger thrill, seeing the Olympics or being the last ones up.

* * * *

Bicycling

Being an active family, used to traveling under our
own steam and most reluctant to confine ourselves to a
car, we sought out the complimentary bicycles our first
morning. A woman led us to a long, low, abundantly
stocked shed filled with bicycles which featured large
handlebars, wide seats, heavy tires, and a general impression of indestructibility, ideal for the rough roads of
Long Island. An hour later we were convinced that
bicycling is the best way to explore many of the Out
Islands. Sparsely populated, predominantly level,
crisscrossed by numerous country roads and scenic, they
offer excellent touring for all ages. While car rentals are
always available, their cost can be prohibitive for budget
travelers and an unnecessary expense. Nor does covering large distances (the only real reason for a car) seem in
keeping with the Bahamas experience. Bicycling
matches the pace of the islands, forcing visitors to abandon their faster lifestyle and savor a slower tempo. The
refreshing exposure of bicycling can teach you much
about the fine art of lingering, of savoring the experience
over the speed at which it was executed.

One morning we planned a trip to Cape Santa Maria,
site of one of the more spectacular beaches to be found.
Eschewing the free transport to the beach offered by the
resort, we arranged instead to bike there and return in
the resort truck with the other guests, thus avoiding too
much mid-day sun. We were all still looking a bit pink,
and Gwyneth would get more than her share of exposure
in her backpack. Following the road through the villages
of Burnt Ground, Clinton's and Seymours, we were
passed infrequently by cars, the passengers grinning and
waving at the sight of our family. The towns themselves
were almost in obscurity, their existence only hinted at

by a tidy, white church, small grocery store, or village school. Pastel homes dotted the roadside, each set in a colorful garden. Vegetable plots, at first invisible, revealed themselves in a wealth of corn and cabbage, tomato and pepper plants, peeping from the tall, untamed vegetation. Scattered citrus trees, bananas and papayas offered tempting visions of ripening fruit. Gardening here is more a matter of planting something where you see a patch of soil, rather than any organized plot. Two banana trees might poke up among a riot of bushes, or a small tomato plot be mixed in among bougainvillea, hibiscus and palms. The homes looked tidy and clean, their painted wooden shutters drawn against the sun and heat, or propped open with a stick. A few sported louvered windows, an obvious sign of prosperity. One village store, larger than the others, drew us to a stop where we found fresh milk, arranging to pick it up on our return. Despite the brisk wind, the sun and heat, the bicycling was easy and enjoyable, a wonderful renewal of our ongoing love affair with the Bahamas. As the children said, "Even the air smells of the Bahamas."

Later, riding on seats in the back of a truck, we realized that so much of what we had seen was missed by vehicle travel—the young woman laundering clothes at the well behind her house; clean clothes blowing on backyard clotheslines; the men hoeing a small vegetable patch from the hard soil; tiny garden plots sprouting up among the seeming disarray of wild vegetation; the tall, stately woman walking down the road, her smooth dress hanging to her calves, hair pulled back in a neat knot tied with a red band, carrying her beautiful baby, its brown face peering from a white, starched bonnet; the school children clad in brown and white uniforms, peeking through open windows at a one-room school. From a vehicle, the surroundings seemed less intimate. While many travelers to a tropical place like the Bahamas seek little more than a relaxing time in the sun, an escape from daily pressures, a touch of luxury living, travelers of an adventurous sort have a different travel experience, mainly because of their attitude. Lured by the chance to discover and reflect, they seek something the average tourist does not—a simpler life-style, a friendlier, more caring sense of community, and an element of self-sufficiency, things that have gradually been weaned from the developed world in the name of progress.

While Long Island is surely one of the best places for bicycling, any of the large Out Islands offer equal opportunities for bicycle touring. As with Long, Cat Island is made for bicycle travel, with its sparse population and almost deserted country roads. For the ultimate biking adventure, a tour of Long or Cat from one end to the other would be exciting. Exuma and Eleuthera could also be enjoyed by bicycle, provided you escaped the main routes and sought backroads. Smaller islands such as Harbour Island and the Abacos are popular places for bicycling, both with tourists and inhabitants. Bikes can usually be rented, either at the resorts or in a nearby town, although we noted their condition rarely matched what we were offered at Stella Maris. Nor are rental bikes necessarily inexpensive. In fact in some locations the cost to outfit a family for the day could approach what you would expect to pay for a rental car.

* * * *

Food Shopping & Bakeries

As a family with two teenage sons, food shopping seems to be a continual focus in our travel. Practically the first thing we seek out at any destination is the nearest food source, even taking priority over a place to spend the night. While most vacationers head for the nearest restaurant, we prowl the streets looking for grocery stores, bakeries, and open-air markets. Why? Because even though eating out occasionally is a welcome treat, nothing stretches the budget more for a traveling family than preparing your own meals.

As usual, we hadn't been on Long Island twenty-four hours before we found our first grocery and bakery. Bakeries seem to abound in the Out Islands. Given the scattered homes, the sparse population, the limited financial resources, it's amazing to find bakeries cropping up at odd turns in the road. Coming from North America, where bakeries in the countryside are practically an anachronism, the sight of one seems like a gift from heaven. We found our first while bicycling home from the beach. It was a small, wooden building situated beside a simple home. Outside stood a well, a plot of pepper and tomato plants nestled among the coral rock, various cats sunning themselves on the doorstep, and a small, smiling girl peering from behind the screen door. Like most other Bahamian children, she was impeccably dressed and clean, her white dress and hair ribbon bright against her smooth, black skin. It's interesting how poverty often lends itself to pride in appearance, something we've encountered in other developing countries. At home, despite our washing machines and dryers, our abundance of clothes and comparative wealth, children tend to look twice as grubby. Here, the women and girls wear dresses, very clean and attractive, with the women's hair drawn neatly back in a smooth knot. Men and boys typically wear long trousers and button-down shirts.

Inside the bakery was a simple wooden room, with one long counter displaying loaves of fresh white bread and jars filled with sugar cookies. An elderly woman presided, exuding the charm that seems to be a national characteristic, urging our children to try her "Bennies", a cookie made from locally-produced sesame seeds. We savored, purchased, lingered and socialized, all standard procedure when island shopping.

Bakeries like this are found throughout the Out Islands, small places usually operating out of someone's home. Hours vary, as do locations and the things they sell, but all produce fresh loaves of bread that prove almost irresistible. To locate one, ask at the tourist bureau (if there is one), the hotel you're staying at, or just someone on the street. A few sell whole wheat bread, usually on a limited basis. As one woman told us, "It don't sell so good." Some have a reputation for certain goodies: the cinnamon buns at Sawyers on Man-O-War, Vernon's whole wheat bread in Hope Town, Mom's muffins in George Town. If you are traveling with children, a visit to a bakery can be as big a treat as an ice cream, particularly if your family isn't accustomed to home baking. And the presence of your young will work like magic on the Bahamians, all of whom seem to be equally enamored of children.

Food shopping is generally easy in the Out Islands once you know what to look for. Every community has at least one food shop, sometimes more. Seemingly limited at first glance, they can reveal quite a variety once you delve into their compact quarters. We found the same basic foods we find throughout the world: cheese, canned fish, rice, beans, pasta, eggs, butter, cereal, raisins, baby food, crackers, cookies, potatoes, cabbage, onions, carrots, bananas, peanuts, even peanutbutter. Specialty foods like fresh produce, juice and fresh milk are dependent on the mailboat and tend to run out midweek. Tinned and powdered whole milk are always available. Variety varies tremendously between the limited supply on Cat and Long to the supermarket quality of places like George Town and Marsh Harbour. Prices are high no matter where you shop, as most foodstuff first comes to Nassau from Europe or the United States, then by mailboat to the islands. Food costs are accepted as part of Out Island life. Prices are lowest in the Abacos where many products come directly from the States.

At Stella Maris we discovered a well-stocked store an easy mile from the resort, selling everything from eggs to kerosene lamps. If you are bicycling, the maze of paved roads, remnants of aborted development plans in the '60s, can be a bit confusing. It's best to get good directions from the resort. We didn't, and in desperation finally resorted to an illegal nip across the airport runway before finding our way. Good buys at the store include cheese, carrots, bananas, cookies and crackers (an English variety!). Another day, bicycling to Cape Santa Maria, we tried a couple of food shops, which ranged from a humble dwelling to a veritable supermarket. Bahamian shop owners are endlessly obliging, seeking out items, holding food purchases for later pick-up, or directing you to another store to find a desired product.

* * * *

Beaches

While every Bahamian island has beaches, Long Island has some of the best: long stretches of fine white sand washed by the sun and gentle, "Caribbean side" waves; tiny ocean-side pockets of perfect beach nestled between raw outcroppings of coral rock; beaches that lie shaded under casuarinas or baked by the sun. Some beckon irresistibly along the quiet roadside or lie secretly in hidden corners. All share the common bond of unspoiled splendor, gifts of nature that still exist for their own sake rather than the whim of man.

Our first morning we sought out Deal's Beach, located an easy five miles away. Although there are plenty of sandy areas for sunning or children's play at Stella Maris, the rocky, wave-swept ocean shore keeps swimmers at bay. Instead, free transport is provided daily to either Deal's or Cape Santa Maria, a gorgeous beach ten miles north. The bicycle ride was easy and level to Deal's, involving the usual number of detours—the general store for picnic food, the small marina for complimentary fins, plus assorted wrong turns that led to much hilarity. Gwyneth slept the whole way in her backpack as we passed the bakery, a community well, the village school and scattered homes in varying stages of disrepair. The beach itself is a lovely strip of perfect Bahamas sand, with three resort-owned sailboats, a cabana, picnic table, and generally no one there. We found the close proximity of the road was no problem as cars were rare. We did it all—sailing, swimming, snorkeling, picnicking. Gwyneth Islay, fascinated by the fine sand, bathed herself (and me) in it. Stripped naked, except for her sunhat, she turned brown before our eyes. So much for people's fears that sunscreen interferes with tanning. Aided by SPF#30, Gwyneth Islay got the best tan of all.

Another day we bicycled to Cape Santa Maria beach, arranging with the resort truck to pick us up for the return trip. Located to the north of Stella Maris, the beach is spectacular in a way only the Bahamas can provide—a long crescent of white sand edged with casuarinas, dunes and scrub growth, curving around a bay of clear, turquoise water; one anchored cruising boat, a small resort at the far end, and the silence of nature. Reached by a pothole-ridden dirt and coral rock affair that doubles as a road, it remains lovely and undisturbed. Like all other Bahamian beaches, it is open to the public, but we found only the half-dozen people who took the free ride from Stella Maris for a morning in the sun. Sharing a four-mile beach with a few others generates more of a feeling of camaraderie than one of imposition. Instead of indulging our usual compulsion for striking out on our own, we found ourselves lingering to socialize. The paradox was striking, for it is urban places that tend to make us anti-social, the sheer numbers of people causing the rejection. Experiencing each other in small groups in rural settings, we regain our social equanimity.

* * * *

Beach Tar

There is a down side to ocean-side beaches in the Bahamas, an aspect that the country itself bears little responsibility for. That is the tar and trash that wash up on the islands' lovely shores. The trash comes mostly from the passing cruise ships. Somehow the dichotomy of pampered guests and littered beaches both springing from the same source is especially powerful, significant of man's often-conflicting habits. While creating an aura of perfection on board ship, they simultaneously create a rubbish pile on shore. Trash generated by the so-called "luxury" cruise ship is heaved overboard in the dead of night while guests sleep in blissful ignorance. As with simple conveniences such as trash pick-up service or flush toilets, it fosters an out-of-sight, out-of-mind mentality.

Far worse than trash, something that can easily be removed, is the beach tar, washed ashore from countless flushed holds of passing oil tankers. Tar on many of the outer beaches of the Bahamas is a fact of life (tar is not found on the Caribbean-side beaches). While it can usually be easily avoided, some hotels in the Bahamas post signs and leave materials on hand for tar removal from feet (anything with an oil base, such as sunscreen, baby oil, mayonnaise, and so on).

One day, while walking Gwyneth in her backpack for a nap, I saw Kevin and the boys working industriously on a small beach at Stella Maris. While the boys fetched and carried with ant-like devotion, Kevin knelt on the beach playing artisan. Calling on latent talents, and using the medium at hand, he fashioned a small tar baby, one worthy of an Uncle Remus story. The result was impressive, creative, a source of entertainment for the children. Beneath its frivolity, however, lurked a darker side—the very existence of his tar baby was disturbing, a reminder of the far-reaching impact of our social habits on an otherwise pristine setting.

* * * *

Travels With Baby:
The Case of the Disappearing Diapers

It was only our second day in the Bahamas that our travels took an unprecedented turn. Traveling with a baby, we knew from experience, is amusing, lively, and guaranteed to keep you on your toes. There's little lounging at the beach or lingering over cups of coffee and decadent desserts, no indulgent lazy mornings in bed or hours spent with your nose in a book. Gwyneth, fortunately, was turning out to be a traveling trooper, for the most part unfazed by her changing routine, domicile, and social circle. Our second day, however, was an epic one in the annals of traveling with a baby. While accompanying Kevin and me at a morning coffee-hour meeting with Peter, one of the proprietors of Stella Maris, she played happily with the spoons, crawled under the table, cooed coyly, and was finally borne off by one of the dining room staff in the direction of the kitchen. All was well until I heard her cry, followed by the help returning bearing a tearful baby in one arm and a plate in the other. The crumbs on Gwyneth's mouth revealed the problem. The poor woman had given our babe a bit of pound cake. Imagine her surprise when instead of happily gobbling it up and demanding more, Gwyneth Islay burst into tears and gagged. Fortunately, she saved the final indignity until she was safely in my lap. Gwyneth, poor dear, had never had solid food. Kevin, naturally, thoroughly enjoyed the cake in the aftermath.

Later that same day, as I was changing the baby after a bicycle ride and looking around for her bag of dirty diapers, I realized it had disappeared. Even if this island had a theft problem (which it doesn't—even the villas have no locks on the doors), I doubt that fifteen dirty diapers would be high priority stolen goods. Only one of two things could have happened: either the maid threw them away (hard to confuse a heavy bag of dirty diapers with trash), or she had sent them to be laundered (God forbid—the price would be exorbitant!). Whichever or whatever, half my diaper supply had disappeared, a less than desirable state of affairs on my second day of two months in a country where the local women practically bribe you to bring them good cloth diapers from the States.

Thus launched probably the first dirty diaper search ever undertaken at Stella Maris. We trotted down to the laundry ("No, Mam, there's no diapers here"), into the bowels of the trash shed (we could see only cases of empty bottles), and finally home, assured that nothing more could be done until the maid came in the next morning and solved the mystery. Of course, whether she came in time to save them from suffering the fate of all departing trash seemed a bit unsure. Calling her was out of the question. Long Island homes often have no electricity, much less working telephones. In fact, the word "working" is a key one there. As Peter frequently said with a smile about things that didn't work, "We're working on it."

The climax to the episode took place as Kevin, the children and I were taking an evening walk. Up drove the "Boss Lady", as the help called her, pulling to a stop alongside us in her open jeep. There, nestled beside her on the passenger seat, sat my diaper bag, looking at this stage a bit smutty. Taking matters into her own hands, she had initiated another, more successful search of the trash bins, finally unearthing them under a heap of rubbish. As recompense, she offered to have them laundered for free, a service we accepted with alacrity. Breathing a sigh of relief, we noticed our sons' reaction was more practical. "Maybe we could arrange to have the maid throw them away every time we need them washed," they suggested impishly.

*   *   *   *

Great Exuma

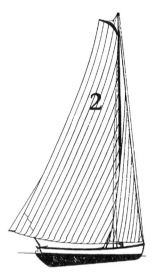

With flat, sun-baked, white sand beaches, this yachting center of the southern Bahamas is eager to develop and struggling to keep abreast with the twentieth century. Around each corner seems to be a new home, a road under construction, a planned resort, although the pace remains slow, the results negligible. George Town is teaming with sailors and an element of action. If you are coming from Long Island or Cat, it feels like the height of civilization; from Florida, the ends of the earth.

Island Hopping

We left Long Island on a note of regret, having barely scratched the surface of what we wanted to see and do. That always seems to be the way on our trips, not matter how long we stay, how much we do, how many people we meet. Even islands, defined by their more manageable size, remain large in experience; too large to fully explore in one visit. Bahamian Out Islands, among the smallest, seem to grow larger through exposure. There's no absolute solution, for traveling by car in order to "see" everything deprives one of the more meaningful, rewarding experience of lingering in one place. Only continual exposure allows a glimpse under the surface of things, a feeling that somehow you've touched the heart of a place.

The trip to Great Exuma, the nearest neighboring island, involved another small airplane for the forty mile hop. This one, a six-seater (lucky we don't have a bigger family) owned and operated by Stella Maris resort, was the biggest on the island. It was piloted by Peter's son, a brusque, efficient type with little of the mellowing of age that so characterizes his charming father.

Flying between Out Islands is somewhat complex and fairly expensive at best. Bahamasair, the national airline company, operates all their domestic flights through Nassau, a process that can involve hundreds of miles of travel just to reach a neighboring island. Worse yet, some inter-island travel through Nassau requires an overnight stop between flights, an added inconvenience and expense. Consequently, places such as Long, Exuma, Cat and Eleuthera have at least one private air charter operator specifically for people trying to get from one Out Island to another. While charter flights are costly, the experience of visiting different islands can be well worth the expense. To accommodate a one-way charter flight, you can easily arrange your roundtrip flight from the U.S. so you arrive on one island and fly home from another. If flying between islands is beyond your budget, limit yourself to one island and save the others for subsequent trips. The Abacos are the one exception, where close proximity between islands has produced an excellent inter-island ferry service.

For those with the time and inclination, the small island mailboats offer a less expensive way to get from one island to another. In most instances it means taking one boat to Nassau and spending a night or two there before finding a boat to your final destination. Schedules and fares are available locally.

* * * *

Taxi Ride

Taxi rides are almost an inevitability on the larger islands. With no public transportation, you're bound to take a taxi sooner or later, even if it's just to and from the airport. Our first ride greeted us upon arrival in Exuma, a necessity if we wanted to cover the twelve miles into George Town and our hotel. The fact that we were also the only potential clients practically precipitated a crisis among the idle cab drivers hovering at the airport door. Although taxis operate on a queue system, there seemed to be some disagreement as to who was actually first in line. Heated words were exchanged and our bags passed back and forth before No. 15 (all Exuma cab drivers are known by their license number) emerged as our driver. Leading us to his vintage Oldsmobile, he went through a series of athletic feats before successfully opening the trunk. Next, the engine was started, an apparent necessity prior to loading passengers. Once inside, Gwyneth made valiant efforts to eat the dusty seatbacks, while the rest of us battled with the closed windows. No.15's vehicle clearly had the Bahamian taxi cab seal of approval—an exhaust system that vented through the back seat.

The road into town was flat, had numerous potholes, and seemed to be under a perpetual state of construction.

Coconut Cove Hotel, George Town

Reservations:	809-336-2659
Direct Phone:	809-336-2659
Direct Fax:	809-336-2658

Location: Just north of George Town on Great Exuma.

Accommodations: 20-person capacity in nine hotel rooms and one large suite with hot tub.

Getting There: Take a commercial flight from Miami, Ft. Lauderdale or Nassau to George Town, Exuma; take a taxi to the Coconut Cove Hotel on the outskirts of town.

Local Transport: Resort shuttle service to town and taxis.

Meals: Either MAP, EP or by the meal; non-guests welcome at the hotel's fine restaurant.

Amenities: There is a pool with water access to the bar area, a good restaurant, a water taxi service to the beaches of Stocking Island, a mini-van shuttle service to town, and a laundry service.

Phones: There is a direct line at front desk and pay phones located throughout George Town.

Electricity: Great Exuma has reliable utility electricity.

Water: Water in rooms is drinkable, although there is a slight mineral taste; bottled water is also available.

Laundry: The Coconut Cove Hotel has a laundry service and there are two laundromats in George Town.

Food Stores & Restaurants: In town is the Exuma Market and M & L Quality Meats, the Towne Cafe bakery, Mom's mobile bakery, the Two Turtles Inn barbecue on Tuesday and Friday evenings, and several other restaurants.

Highlights:

- A small hotel on the outskirts of George Town, the Coconut Cove Hotel enjoys both relatively quiet surroundings and easy access to town.

- Originally a private home, the hotel evolved into the attractive, intimate place it is today.

- The hotel grounds are small and the road to town is nearby, but the gardens and the fish pond with arched bridge are nice touches.

- The rooms have small outdoor decks or terraces. Some of the rooms overlook the harbor and Stocking Island in the distance.

- The hotel is situated on a quiet cove north of George Town. The beach is nice and the shallow waters good for bone fishing in season.

- Scheduled hotel transport is available to and from town, although walking is also possible.

- The small restaurant has a well-deserved reputation for gourmet food and good service.

- The outdoor deck-side pool has a circular bar built into one end of it.

"First the government put in water. Now they put in telephone," the driver explained. Unfortunately, they didn't put them in together, or on the same side of the street. Coupled with the fact that pavement in the Bahamas peaks at about a half inch thick, you could see it was going to be some time before travel approached anything close to normality.

Homes seemed to be springing up like weeds, catering to a growing population of expatriate American and European sun-seekers. Cars were far more plentiful than on Long Island, many of them roaring by with what sounded like defunct mufflers. What the trip lacked in aesthetic appeal it made up for in social entertainment. Taxi drivers, like most other Bahamians, are social creatures, ready to provide answers (even to questions you didn't ask), give tours, and generally go out of their way to make you feel welcome. Nor are they motivated by profit alone. In the course of our trip drivers made detours, helped locate stores, waited while we shopped, and once even hand-delivered groceries we mistakenly left in the vehicle. No. 15 seemed particularly solicitous, perhaps because we had a baby. Having successfully negotiated the twelve rugged miles, he turned into the entrance of our hotel and pulled up behind a parked van.

"We can just get out here," Kevin offered, reaching for the door handle.

"No, man. It's a long way yet. You wait here," the driver insisted. We waited, picturing a long drive, banks of flowers, towering palms, a gracious entrance. Finally the van in front started up and pulled away. Easing the Olds into gear, No.15 inched a car's length forward, then stopped. Turning around, he grinned with pleasure. "Here we are."

* * * *

Yachties

George Town, the hub of Great Exuma, is a town of yachtsmen. Being avid sailors ourselves, we still found their presence a bit overwhelming, but then our visit coincided with the annual week-long Cruising Regatta, not to be confused with the Out Islands Regatta featuring traditional Bahamian craft held later in the spring. The combination of well-protected harbor, jumping-off spot for the Caribbean, and excellent facilities makes George Town a natural haven for yachties, particularly those who like company in numbers and plenty of social activities. We met sailing families whose disgruntled teenagers came to life upon arrival. One sailor's wife, new to the world of boats, was thrilled with the community atmosphere, a far cry from the deserted anchorages and remote feeling that typifies most of Bahamas cruising. Other more independent types find the social scene overpowering. As one woman remarked, "I don't need a social director to go cruising."

The social scene peaks during Cruising Regatta week, with hundreds of boats at anchor and organized activities ranging from sailboat races and beach games to cocktail parties and a peas-n'-rice-eating contest. The latter, the Bahamian version of the old pie-eating standby, took place at the Two Turtles Inn (a popular hangout with yachties), where a variety of participants attempted to gobble down bowls of the Bahamian national dish with record-breaking gusto. Given the "go" signal, one table of amply-endowed ladies revealed that what they were really there for was a free meal. Ignoring the frantic culinary activities of their neighbors, they proceeded to eat with a leisured pace. Another group, this time athletic-looking young men with winners' physiques, buckled quickly under the onslaught of fried rice. At the children's table, a petite young girl displayed an unbeatable technique, putting to shame the larger teenagers who struggled to keep abreast. It didn't take long to pinpoint the future winner, a short, round, red-headed young man. Barely coming up for air, he relentlessly forced bowl after bowl down his throat. Like all speed-eating contests, this one bordered on the grotesque, particularly when it came to the dog entries. Primed and spurred on by their owners, these canine yachties polished off enough peas-n'-rice to keep a Bahamian family in food for a week.

* * * *

George Town Facilities

Given its remote location in the Bahamas, George Town offers just about anything you might need—excellent grocery stores, laundromats, bakeries, restaurants, boat supplies, marina facilities, tourist shops, even an information bureau. For provisioning during your travels, you can't do better anywhere in the Out Islands south of Marsh Harbor, Abaco, the other major Out Island facilities center. While people who like solitude and natural surroundings will prefer limiting their stay to a brief stocking-up or laundering of clothes, more sociable creatures will find its friendly, low-key nightlife a welcome entertainment. Social centers include the Peace & Plenty, the Two Turtles Inn, with its al fresco seating and bar, and Sam's Place, a cafe/restaurant overlooking the marina. The social hub of the town, however, seems to be the Exuma Market, with a continual swarm of yachties converging daily in their quest for food and ice. Another store, located a few minutes' walk away, remains blissfully uncrowded, due to its greater distance from the dinghy dock. An open-air market, the only one of its kind we were to find in the Out Islands, offers a wide variety of produce at excellent prices. As always in the Out Islands, variety is best after the weekly mailboat delivery. For baked goods there is a bakery in town and "Mom's", a venerable local lady who sells home baked goodies from her van. Judging from the enthusiastic hugs, kisses and greetings she receives on a daily basis, it's obvious that Mom is a George Town landmark.

Laundry can be done at one of several laundromats in town. With water a precious commodity, machines only rinse once and fill at an almost imperceptible rate. The first time I used one of the machines, I thought it had stuck permanently on rinse.

With no town beach and few local places for children to play, the best way for an active family to enjoy a stay in George Town is to rent a motorboat. A boat gives you unlimited access to good beaches and fishing grounds, and is ideal for coastal explorations.

* * * *

Stocking Island

Long, undeveloped, lined with white sand beaches, Stocking Island helps form the large protected harbor George Town is noted for. Sailors anchored off the island usually bring their boat across for supplies rather than make the trip in a dinghy. Tourists have the option of either renting a motorboat or using the ferry service provided by a few of the hotels. The Peace & Plenty has a twice-daily service in a dependable looking boat. The Coconut Cove Hotel, located just outside of town, supplies free morning rides to hotel guests, a convenience

Kevin encouraged the children and me to take advantage of one day while he went to town on business. A ten o'clock departure time was arranged with Arthur, the tall, lanky young Bahamian who served as general factotum at the hotel.

Ten o'clock rolled around and no Arthur. At about ten-thirty he appeared, looking as if he was early, if anything. That's just doing things on Bahamian time. We climbed aboard the docked Boston Whaler, with Gwyneth in the Snugli, the beach bag, mats, towels and snorkeling gear. My nautical eye had already perceived the rather wild conditions in the harbor, the result of a brisk wind coming straight out of the southeast. White caps and waves somewhat dampened my ardor for a beach outing, particularly with a baby and traveling in a small boat that seemed to be shrinking fast. Being a sailor, my faith in engines has never been great. What little confidence remained vanished as Arthur made several unsuccessful attempts to start the engine. Tom, the hotel owner who was watching from the dining deck, came hurrying down upon the scene to show Arthur the proper technique. The more advice he gave, the more incompetent Arthur became, until it looked as though only a miracle would get us across the harbor. Colin, all sympathy with Arthur, said that's the way he feels when a grown-up is criticizing him—instead of improving the situation, it makes him more inept than ever.

Heading out, I noticed that waves which had looked unpleasant from on shore were taking on alarming proportions up close. Worse yet, they all seemed hell-bent on coming aboard. No sooner had we left our cove than they began sweeping across the bow. As we were also all seated in the aforementioned bow, we soon started to get wet. I had the foresight to wrap Gwyneth in a beach towel, Snugli and all. Lulled by the motion and insulated from the elements, she fell asleep within seconds for the duration of the trip. Tristan, poor boy, found himself in the wettest seat, and was soon thoroughly drenched. In addition to the wind and waves, I now also noticed that Arthur seemed to be picking a dubious course between two small islands up ahead. "You don't think he's planning to go between them, do you?" I remarked to the children. We might have known. He was.

Once away from the dock, Arthur did an admirable job at the helm. We made the trip in good time, wind, waves, small boat and all. Stocking Island was well worth the trip, with a lovely beach all to ourselves, warm water, hot sun, and no end of things for the children to do. Tristan and Colin soon devised makeshift boats from pieces of wood, while Gwyneth Islay exhibited a new level of beach bravery, venturing to the water's edge. Even the return trip was pleasant, with the waves at our back quarter and Arthur exhibiting a positive aura of competence.

* * * *

A Change Of Plans

In the interests of our research, we were booked to stay at three different places on Great Exuma. The first and last were in or around George Town, while the second hotel, where our booking was as yet unconfirmed, was fifteen miles up-island past the airport. Due to poor planning, we would have to cover the distance between George Town and the airport vicinity no less than four times, a unwelcome expense in terms of taxi fares. Everything else in town was thoroughly booked because of the influx of visitors for Cruising Regatta Week. Kevin had his hands full trying to work out a contingency plan in the event that the second hotel didn't have rooms reserved for us. Our only hope seemed to be a vague possibility of an apartment for rent nearby the hotel, suggested by a charming American woman named Jeannine, who had befriended Gwyneth one day at Sam's Place.

Since he was having trouble contacting the second hotel, Kevin enlisted the help of our hotel manager at the Coconut Cove, a competent British woman named Valerie. She attempted to communicate by CB with Junior, a taxidriver who apparently lived out near the hotel. "Junior!", she called in her imperious British tones. "Junior! Come in, please!" Junior tried, but the static that appears to plague all radio communication on Exuma drowned him out. Valerie persisted, with Junior making garbled responses for the next five minutes; then the whole radio suddenly went dead. Glancing out her window, Valerie jumped. "Oh God!", she exclaimed. "Here comes Junior now." Sure enough, there he was, walking up the drive. Junior had been sitting in his taxi right next door the whole time.

"Sure, the hotel is open," he replied, when told of our difficulties. "No phone, though." So that was the problem. "And you can't get any dinner," he added as an afterthought.

Kevin felt like asking if there was any running water. The prospects of a delightful visit were not encouraging, even if they did have rooms for us.

Next, in a valiant attempt to stay within our limited writer's budget, Kevin tried to secure a ride in something other than a taxi. A number of people suggested contacting Christine Rolle, a local island woman who lived out past our destination. She came into town daily and might be able to give us a ride. An enterprising Bahamian, she runs a local taxi service and island tour business, as well as markets her book on bush medicine with a persistence that would garner the admiration of any salesperson. Locating Christine proved easy. Going on recommendation, we found her in the lobby at the Peace & Plenty, dressed impeccably in her chauffeur's outfit, driving cap perched atop her wild array of black curls. Pining her down was another issue, as Christine maintained a steady flow of conversation, speaking into her walkie-talkie while simultaneously carrying on a conversation with three hovering tourists. Kevin finally made contact, establishing that she would pick us up on the way home after her midday island tour at around two. By Bahamian time, that meant anytime between two-thirty and three.

That afternoon evolved into a waiting odyssey. We vacated our room by eleven, parked our bags on the front porch of the hotel and removed ourselves to the pool deck to await Christine's arrival. We lunched, briefly dipped, chatted to other guests, wandered down to the Peach & Plenty Beach Club for a tea and coffee, read, nursed the baby, and generally did our best to stave off boredom. At three-thirty we served up bowls of cereal with milk for our ravenous children, which coincided perfectly with Christine's arrival. Because the last time we'd met she had evinced no interest in doing anything quickly, and since she was now over an hour late, we were taken aback to see her leap out of her van and start flinging our bags inside with reckless abandon. Ominous mutterings spewed from her lips. "Hurry! Hurry!," she exclaimed. Given the circumstances, this was hardly what we expected.

Once we were safely ensconced inside her vintage van, she drove off with an ear-shattering grinding of gears.

"I've got no clutch," she shot back at us over the noise.

Seawatch Ocean Villas, Great Exuma

Reservations:	802-626-9333
Phone (US office):	802-626-5233
Fax (US office):	802-626-9335

Location: Great Exuma, 13 miles north of George Town and a few miles north of the airport

Accommodations: (2) 2-bedroom and (4) 1-bedroom apartments available on short term lease or by the day.

Getting There: Take a commercial flight from Miami, Ft. Lauderdale or Nassau to George Town, Exuma; rent a car at the airport or take a taxi to the Seawatch Ocean Villas (you might want to go to town for food first).

Local Transport: Rental cars, intermittent bus service to George Town, and taxis.

Meals: Cooking facilities are provided.

Amenities: Kitchen-living room; bath; bedroom(s); porch; electricity; outdoor shower.

Phones: In the manager's apartment; pay phones in town.

Electricity: Great Exuma has reliable utility electricity.

Water: Water in the apartments is drinkable.

Laundry: Laundromats and laundry service in George Town.

Food Stores & Restaurants: most stores and restaurants are located in and around George Town, although there is a food store a few miles north of the villas on the Queen's Highway.

Highlights:

- This is a good choice for visitors to Great Exuma seeking privacy, independence and completely natural surroundings.

- The villas have an abundance of privacy and solitude.

- There is an amazing beach with good swimming and snorkeling right in front of the villas.

- There are great walks down the small roads in the surrounding area.

- Wooden steps lead down to one of the best beaches you could hope to find, shared only with a handful of seasonal residents.

- The one or two bedroom apartments have plenty of room for a family, with good kitchen facilities with dining area and ample living area.

Her clutch, it seemed, had given out during the latter stages of her latest island tour, leaving her in a raging hurry to get to her mechanic. We took the twelve miles back to the airport in record time, flying over the bumps, cracks and crevices while the engine screamed in low gear. A few miles farther she pulled up alongside the road and announced this was our hotel, and could we please get out fast before her engine stalled. As if on cue, her engine sputtered, petered out, and died, thus allowing us to at least unload with some degree of dignity. While Kevin and the boys gave her a push and waved her down the road, I took stock of the surroundings. The overgrown vegetation and dilapidated buildings were decidedly below par for a Bahamian resort. We soon learned what the problem was—the hotel was in the process of changing ownership and was going through a rather painful "transition phase". We seemed to be the only guests and there wasn't even running water. The hotel manager who locked up and went home at night told us that rooms were available (it appeared the entire hotel was available). There had to be something better than this.

"What about Jeannine?" I suggested to Kevin. "She said she lived nearby and knew about those rental apartments." Since it was late in the day, Kevin was all for waiting until tomorrow until I literally forced him out the door. Dutifully, he and the children ventured forth, leaving me to nurse the baby. For the next half hour the baby slept and I contemplated my surroundings.

Meanwhile, Kevin was walking down the road reassuring the children that staying at the hotel for the night would be just like camping. If I'd been there I would have set him straight. Staying in a deserted, rundown hotel with no water is not like camping. I tried comparing it to the truly memorable place we stayed in outside Tafraoute in Morocco. Why did I find one adventurous and the other depressing? It was clear—the hotel in Morocco was a normal circumstance for a small mountain village in that country, while this was decidedly irregular for the Bahamas.

Unbeknownst to me, the boys and Kevin had arrived at Jeannine's place and presented our case. Jeannine, ever helpful, called the caretaker of the apartments who said he'd be right over. As if on cue, his pickup truck materialized in her driveway.

The first I knew of all this was the sylvan sounds of a truck roaring in and pulling up outside our door. To say that my hopes weren't up would have been the gravest lie. The children came bursting in, grabbing everything in sight, exclaiming that we were leaving that instant.

The small apartment complex was literally around the corner, just off a quiet road, overlooking the water and an exquisite beach. One bedroom with a double bed, bathroom (with water!), hall, and main room with hide-a-bed couch, dining table, chairs...and kitchen! We were ecstatic. Outside was a stone terrace with chairs, and a wooden boardwalk leading down to the beach. Overhead fans kept the rooms cool, while the refrigerator and stove seemed like a gift from the gods.

Colin immediately grabbed a broom, while Tristan followed up with a wet mop, cleaning the floor for Gwyneth. The tea kettle was put on to boil and Kevin appeared proudly bearing an irreplaceable gift: a box of minute brown rice he'd bought from our neighbors, thus putting the seal on a totally successful extrication from a bad scene. The only other residents were a Bahamian couple with two children, Cyril the manager, and Art and Isabelle, a charming retired couple from New Jersey (and the source of the brown rice). Art showed up as we were making dinner bearing a loaf of homemade (by him) zucchini-nut-raisin bread. We dined royally on what was our first home-cooked meal of the trip.

Dinnertime conversation revolved around the joys of having our own place, of not being dependent on others, of being out in the countryside, of living with more than one room, and of being able to cook. Other families visiting for just a week or so undoubtedly welcome the escape from household chores, but for us, on our longer visit, creating a homelike essence from time to time was a welcome respite from the very different atmosphere of a hotel or resort. Other families we met along the way, particularly ones with small children, often shared this sentiment, usually preferring a house or villa rental to staying in a hotel room. As one mother put it, "That way I can feed the children at all those odd hours they seem to get hungry."

We truly appreciated the hospitality of Art, the efficiency of our apartment, and the pure good fortune of having met Jeannine at Sam's Place. "Gwyneth saves the day again," Colin proclaimed. It was true. Jeannine only approached us because she wanted to see the baby. We all gave Gwyneth Islay appropriate hugs and kisses. She not only provided entertainment, but solutions as well.

People often ask us "What if...?". It's amazing how "what if" scenarios always seem to lead to their own solutions, provided one recognizes them. The moral of this is never be afraid to make a move when your instincts tell you to, to instigate a change of plans or cancel something altogether. Not only will the end result be worth the added effort, but it will often lead to some of your most unexpected experiences and delightful travel memories.

* * * *

Walks

For those who enjoy the pleasures of walking, the
Out Islands offer numerous opportunities. While bicycling had been the preferred mode of travel on Long
Island (who could resist the lure of free bikes?), we soon
found ourselves looking for good walks on Exuma.
Although George Town has little walking other than
strolls around the town, the countryside surrounding
our apartment in Mt. Thompson proved a walker's
paradise. Similar to what we had found at Stella Maris,
the handful of small country roads were remnants of a
planned development started in the late sixties. Judging
from the mere smattering of homes (mostly the winter
retreats of retired Americans), the development urge
hadn't really taken hold. Walking seemed popular
among the residents: the woman with her energetic
cockerspaniel "Sarah"; the two ladies together, one of
whom was a writer and a champion name-dropper; the
young Bahamian on his way to work who implied he
would be happy to play hookey if Kevin and the boys
wanted to go fishing; Art and Isabelle, out for their pre-
breakfast stroll. Everyone was pleasant, eager to talk,
and appreciative of the quiet, natural surroundings, a far
cry from George Town. Their biggest fear was a possible
mega-development in the next cove, complete with
marina, golf course, hotel, and homes. I had already met
a young woman who was both the wife and daughter-in-
law of two of the developers. Telling me of her one visit
to the proposed development site, she remarked that she
wouldn't be going back. "It's all so beautiful. I asked
them why they wanted to go and ruin it."

The views were lovely, out across the sound to the
east, where a steady stream of sailboats could be seen
going to and from George Town. Gorgeous white sand

beaches lay sandwiched between outcroppings of rough coral rock. The waves were gentle, the water turquoise blue. Low vegetation lined the road on either side, the delicate hues of tiny wildflowers almost lost in the bright green of the bushes. Large clumps of sea grape spread their waxy, red-veined, flat leaves of brilliant green. Palmettos reached their long, pointed strands above the low shrubbery. Tallest of all were the scattering of coconut palms and isolated clusters of casuarina pines. Only the sounds of nature pierced the silence: the breaking of waves on the shore, the quick scurrying of lizards along the road or up a stone wall, the low twittering of birds, punctuated by the loud, versatile song of mockingbirds. In a place of such subtle beauty and tranquillity, walking became an island celebration.

* * * *

A Ride To Town

Once again, departure day rolled around, necessitating yet another ride back into George Town. Kevin had made arrangements with Cyril to take us at what Cyril called "dinnertime", something he defined as between five and six. Our faith in his reliability was somewhat shaken by his complete absence all day, despite having assured us he would be around. "Around" was turning out to be a loosely defined term that meant somewhere, anywhere, on the island. By six in the evening, Kevin walked to Jeannine's house to call and confirm our reservation at the Two Turtles Inn. The last thing we needed was to arrive late and find our room had been given away. Jeannine was no more informed about Cyril's whereabouts than we were, but strongly suspected he'd been working on her car at his shop all day.

As the evening progressed, we packed, napped the baby, read—and waited. Isabelle provided some entertainment by appearing and asking if we had electricity, as they didn't and Art's bread was in the oven. Well, Art's bread (all three loaves) was soon in ours, permeating the air with delicious smells. By six-thirty it was out again, being devoured by both households. By seven we were breaking out the last of the food, somewhat slim pickings at this point. By seven-thirty Kevin was back at Jeannine's, this time to discover that, no, Cyril hadn't been at his shop after all. In fact, the chances of getting to George Town were looking pretty slim, especially as it was Sunday and even the few taxis that made it out that way were no longer operating. Fully packed, and with no food in the house, we were beginning to get a bit anxious.

At eight a truck pulled in, bearing our neighbor Clifford Dean, and what we had previously thought was his wife and children (aged three years and three weeks!). No, Art and Isabelle informed us. Children, yes; wife, no. His wife lived in town, as did his six other children. An enterprising man of middle age, Clifford seemed to have a finger in many pies. Kevin cleverly "bumped" into him, strategically brought the conversation around to our plight, and soon had secured a ride for us at 9 o'clock into town. Clifford, it appeared, was returning to town after a brief visit.

Art and Isabelle finally waved us off before taking over our apartment in their quest for light. Their food had long since taken over our refrigerator. Kevin, Gwyneth and I sat up front while the boys rode in the back. Clifford turned out to be quite a character, keeping up a marathon dialogue as he carefully negotiated the ten miles of rugged road. Particularly smitten with Gwyneth, he poked playfully at her. "I love children," he declared. "I just love children. Anyone's children. I've got eight of my own," he added. Next, he moved on to the subject of Cyril. "Why Cyril, he's out fishing. You know, that Cyril, he's got so much on his mind, he's just gone and forgotten about taking you to town." After practically learning Cyril's life story, and how they were like brothers, we moved onto Clifford himself. "I like helping people. Why, I've helped so many people, you wouldn't believe. Thing is, helping people just comes natural to me, you know? It's just my nature."

To top off the ride, we discussed Clifford's prowess as owner and pilot of a charter plane, the one most likely to fly us to Cat Island. We learned what he flew, where he flew, and how he'd put the other charter operator out of business, not because he did a better job, but because he was nicer. It was an enlightening ride.

Arriving at the Two Turtles Inn, we were handed a key and waved in the direction of a room by the bartender. Kevin lingered at the bar to buy Clifford a thank-you drink while the children and I sought out the room. No crib, a tile floor and a scarcity of pillows and towels made fashioning a bed for Gwyneth a bit difficult. We finally threw together everything we could get our hands on—bedspreads, sleeping bags, beach towels, diapers, even violin cases. By now, everyone was exhausted except the baby. Fully rested from her nap, she was positively wired for action, spending the next half hour crawling all over me in bed, pulling my hair , and screeching with delight. Finally she collapsed, nursed, and fell asleep, an appropriate end to what had been an eventful day. One way or another, we had arrived.

* * * *

Travels With Baby:
The Highchair Hijack

Traveling with a hyperactive baby, we were discovering, required a combination of constant vigilance and an increasing need for boundaries. While Tristan and Colin as babies had been habitually confined to a corral (who could chase after twin babies on a regular basis?), the nature of our travels eliminated any such possibility. Nor, we decided, was Gwyneth really the corral type. Mealtimes, on the other hand, needed improvement. No one wanted to spend every meal in a mad chase to keep the baby from courting disaster in her ramblings.

Thus it was that our first sight of a highchair at the Two Turtles Inn was a major cause for celebration. Emerging from our room the first morning, we found an exquisite continental buffet breakfast laid out in the diningroom: fruit juices, toast, jams, homemade muffins, and slices of cake. Inquiries led to the discovery that it was complimentary to all guests, a feature that made the Two Turtles' modest (by Bahamian standards) nightly fee even more economical. Picking a table in the sunshine on the outdoor terrace, we suddenly noticed a highchair in one corner, a grandiose plastic and vinyl affair . Once seated in it, Gwyneth looked like a queen on her infant throne, a vision she immediately dispelled by heaving silverware about in a most unregal fashion. For once, breakfast was a civilized affair, with Gwyneth safely confined to her seat and food, plates, cutlery and cups staying happily on the table. Despite our pride in our ability to do without, our long-standing tradition of lightweight, adaptable travel, the presence of a highchair seemed the height of elegance. Who would have thought that something so basic could have such an impact. We chatted, lingered and luxuriated, reluctant to break the spell of relaxed dining.

Two Turtles Inn, George Town

Reservations:	809-336-2545
Direct Phone:	809-336-2545
Direct Fax:	809-336-2528

Location: In the heart of George Town, Great Exuma

Accommodations: 36-person capacity in twelve rooms, some with kitchens for self-catering.

Getting There: Take a commercial flight from Miami, Ft. Lauderdale or Nassau to George Town, Exuma; rent a car at the airport or take a taxi to the Two Turtles Inn.

Local Transport: Car rentals and taxis.

Meals: The Inn has a nice complimentary continental breakfast on the terrace, lunch specials at the bar and a barbecue Tuesday and Friday evenings.

Amenities: There is a gift store, outdoor bar, restaurant, direct access to town services, some rooms with kitchens, moped and bicycle rentals, fishing and boat charters arranged.

Phones: There is a direct line at the office and pay phones in town.

Electricity: Great Exuma has reliable utility electricity.

Water: The water in the rooms is drinkable, but has a slight mineral taste; bottled water is also available.

Laundry: There are several laundromats and a laundry service in George Town.

Food Stores & Restaurants: Exuma market and M & L Quality Meats, Towne Cafe bakery and Mom's mobile bakery, the Two Turtles Inn barbecues Tuesday and Friday evenings, and several other restaurants in town.

Highlights:

- The hotel has a central location in George Town with access to shopping and nightlife.

- There is a very casual atmosphere, and the Inn has lots of activity both day and night.

- The rooms are built around a central courtyard.

- Comparatively low room rates.

- Bicycle and moped rentals, and good access to boat rentals.

- The complimentary continental breakfast, the nice outdoor bar, and the twice-weekly barbecues.

That night we returned, having discovered the Two Turtles was holding one of its renowned barbecues, destined to warm the heart of any traveling family: barbecued meat, tossed salad, peas-n'-rice, and casual, outdoor seating. The twice-weekly event always drew a crowd of boaters, as well as travelers like ourselves. Looking about for the highchair, we discovered a usurper in it, a small, tow-headed child of indiscriminate age with every indication that she was in no hurry to leave. A Bahamian woman nearby who seemed to be in charge also evinced no hurry in vacating the chair. Gone were our plans of dining with a touch of class.

Finally, with reluctance, the woman rose, removed the offending child, and disappeared into the kitchen bearing the highchair tray. Great, we thought. She's thoughtfully gone to clean it up for our use. After the damage the baby had inflicted, it needed it. Waiting eagerly, we watched as the woman emerged, scooped up the baby, and left, all without any reappearance of the highchair tray. Without it, the chair was useless.

The mystery was solved the next morning. Coming down for breakfast, we discovered the highchair still in its trayless state. As if to avoid any misunderstanding, a curly-headed, blonde three-year-old marched up to our table, precocity and confidence radiating from her miniature person. Clearly the baby's sister, she seemed to be a permanent fixture around the inn.

Undaunted by our adult presence, she peered closely at Gwyneth, making what can best be described as an effort to poke her eyes out. Having satisfied some basic toddler urge, she looked up at me. "You took Rae Dawn's highchair," she announced without preamble. The message was clear. Out of the mouths of babes, so to speak. Our days of civilized dining were over.

*   *   *   *

Cat Island

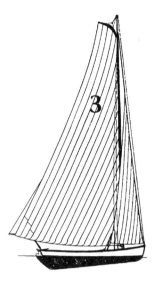

Our arrival on one island was becoming irrevocably linked to our departure from another, in this case a trip on Clifford Dean's airplane. Breaking the mold of operating on Bahamian Time, Clifford appeared at the appointed hour of ten o'clock to drive us from the Two Turtles Inn to the airport. Once again, a ride in his truck came with a liberal dose of Clifford's perspective on life, this time specifically life on Exuma.

"People have forgotten how to make an honest living," Clifford remarked us as we drove along, obliquely referring to the demise of the drug traffic that in the past had nourished many local economies in the Out Islands. "You know what I mean? The economy was good, man, but it made people greedy. Now it's bad, they don't know what to do. But like I said to Cyril when we was talking last night, the system always wins, man. You may be able to beat it a few times, but in the end it always wins." Clifford left us with the impression that he had escaped unscathed, adhering instead to the work ethic that made him the success he clearly was.

At the airport, Clifford led us to his Cherokee six, our smallest plane yet. One engine, I noticed with some trepidation. Even Kevin's iron nerves looked slightly shaken. The boys, however, remained impervious, regarding it as infinitely more adventurous than any jumbo jet. They were right there, I thought, as I observed Clifford going through a series of mysterious flight preparations, none of which looked especially comforting—especially his checking the engine oil and adding a quart or two. Next came the studied business of loading our gear, selecting by size and weight what should go where. Finally we boarded, with Tristan creating a minor disturbance by stepping on the wing flap instead of the wing on his way in.

The Arrival

The arrival at Cat, the island immediately northeast of Exuma, brought us in low over the southern tip of the island, following the line of the coast up to New Bight. From what we could see, there wasn't even a village this far south, nothing except a coastline edged with white sand and an endless expanse of trees. We circled around, then came in smoothly at the airstrip, stopping beside a half-finished building and group of Bahamians only too happy to knock off work and watch the new arrivals. Lining our gear up on a bench in the shade of the building, we sat down to await our ride to the Greenwood Inn.

Twenty minutes later a Plymouth van pulled up, driven by a cheery, middle-aged woman who peered from the window. "Hello," she greeted us. "You must be the Jeffreys. I'm Carolyn." Thus began what was to become one of highlights of our trip, our introduction to Carolyn, her husband Anton, and the Greenwood Inn.

Carolyn, we discovered, was originally from Iowa, a fact that accounted for her friendly, Midwestern-style welcome. Matching Clifford for transportation entertainment, she filled our ears as we set off for the half-hour ride to the inn. Married less than a year (both were widowed), Carolyn and Anton had been managing the Greenwood only since January, an unexpected turn of events brought on by the persistence of the hotel's German owner, Waldemir, a friend of Anton's. "Anton thought he was coming here to do some electrical work," Carolyn explained, with a laugh in her voice, "but when we arrived we discovered Waldemir had fired his manager and wanted us to take over." And how did they like it? "We're having a ball." She gave that impression, her enthusiasm drawing you in and making you feel as though you belonged. Never having been anywhere except Iowa, she was relishing every second, thriving on the constant challenge and ever-changing stimulus of running an island resort, as well as living in a foreign country. During the course of our visit, we noticed that she and her husband had accomplished much in terms of fitting into island life, probably because of their rural farm upbringing. Certainly their open friendliness matched that of the Bahamian temperament, while their sense of responsibility, something that extended to all members of the staff and small community nearby, perfectly suited the intimacy of their rural setting. It wasn't everyone that could so effortlessly make themselves an integral part of a small foreign community in so little time.

Carolyn kept up a running commentary of island life, the sights and facilities nearby, her background, and the history of the Greenwood as we drove south through

Old Bight, then across the island to the east coast. Old Bight was one of those typical strung-out Bahamian towns, with no obvious center other than a small store and one-room school. Tristan and Colin, full of boyish interest regarding the state of the van, remarked on the large external scratch extending down one side, plus the cracked windshield. Carolyn laughed. "A local policeman did that when he was inspecting the van...he was quite embarrassed." It seemed he'd driven into a tree. Why, exactly, was a subject everyone was politely avoiding as negotiations proceeded towards payment—not that anything would happen too fast. After a week on Cat we could see that it would be some time before a new windshield made it that far—if ever.

The scenery we were passing through was exquisite: lush vegetation, a long, thin gleam of sand along the shore, a well-paved road (the best we'd seen on our trip), old, square-built stone houses with open shutters, abundant flowers, even the occasional traditional thatched roof. Small-plot farming still forms the basis of the economy, although the average farmer's age is now sixty-five. Clearly, the young have other things on their mind. Perhaps they would feel differently if marketing techniques were improved, for the Bahamas could benefit from more locally-grown foodstuffs. Prices of imported goods are ridiculous. Carolyn explained she was trying to build up a group of local growers who would provide her regularly, but efficiency is not a Bahamian trademark. Even when produce was available, she couldn't depend on farmers to notify her. In desperation, she'd taken to driving around peering at cultivated fields to determine what was ready for harvest.

Leaving the shore route, we took a rough, uninhabited road across the island to the east coast, then turned down a wide swathe that led to the inn and what was originally planned as a massive, one-thousand-lot housing development. Things being what they are in the Bahamian Out Islands, five houses had been built in the thirty years since its conception. Later, we were shown a plot plan of the original development, a grandiose scheme fabricated by some enterprising entrepreneur and successfully marketed abroad. Taking into consideration the rural landscape, the minimal access and the remoteness of the island, it was incredible to think someone could ever have dreamed this up, let alone sold all the plots. In addition to the one thousand lots, the plan showed a shopping mall, school, park, recreational lake (best identified as the shallow mudhole down the road), even a "Public Beach" located in the middle of a eight-mile uninhabited stretch of sand. Later we were told of a European man who had flown over on a whim to inspect his land purchase. Not having had time to pack for the journey, he figured he could buy what clothes he needed at the shopping mall upon arrival.

* * * *

The Greenwood Inn

The Greenwood Inn was our kind of place on sight—small and intimate, yet catering to those who like independence. An eight mile stretch of perfect sand lay at the inn's doorstep, protected by offshore reefs. Endless places to sit beckoned outdoors: deck chairs and hammocks, beach cabanas and poolside tables. Everywhere were palm trees and flowers, conch shells (with lights hidden inside) lining the paths, stonewalls topped with Portuguese glass fishing balls in nets and ornate shells. Lucky, a large German shepherd, was the resident dog,

The Greenwood Inn, Port Howe

Reservations:	809-342-3053
Direct Phone:	809-342-3053
Direct Fax:	809-342-3053

Location: The inn is located on the southeastern corner of Cat Island on the ocean side.

Accommodations: 44-person capacity in (16) double rooms with king-size beds and (3) 4-person rooms.

Getting There: Take a commercial flight from Miami, Ft. Lauderdale or Nassau (A man on Cat Island also operates a private charter service from Ft. Lauderdale or Nassau); the Greenwood Inn staff will pick you up at the airport.

Local Transport: Resort shuttle service to and from the airport or to interesting local sights.

Meals: Either AP, MAP, EP or by the meal; non-guests are welcome at the hotel restaurant.

Amenities: The Greenwood has a nice pool, bar, restaurant; SCUBA diving, comfortable lounge area, 8-mile beach with snorkeling and swimming in front of the hotel, van service.

Phones: There is a direct line at front desk.

Electricity: The Greenwood Inn generates its own power.

Water: The water in the rooms is drinkable.

Laundry: The hotel has a laundry service.

Food Stores & Restaurants: There is a small market in New Bight with a limited supply of food; a truck comes around periodically with an eclectic assortment of food.

Highlights:

• There are miles and miles of beautiful ocean beaches, great views and comfortable accommodations.

• The rooms are comfortable with king-size beds and small outdoor terraces.

• The inn has a dive shop and there is great diving & snorkeling nearby.

• There is an isolated yet comfortable, relaxing atmosphere in completely natural surroundings.

• The inn is casual and familiar, a place where couples can find solitude and privacy or children can pitch in and help the grounds crew.

• The dinner hour is a lively occasion that brings the guests together for evening socializing.

• There are interesting places in the area to explore.

accompanied by Dolly, Carolyn's pet goat and recent birthday present. The children loved it instantly, recognizing this as the kind of place they could roam and do things at will. For a family destination, it would prove to be unbeatable.

*   *   *   *

Pilot House Excursion

As possessor of one of the few vehicles on southern Cat, Anton was in the habit of picking up anyone alongside the road, as well as ferrying workers to and from the inn, a practice Kevin was indoctrinated into at an early stage of our visit. Hearing that Anton was heading to New Bight to pick up Waldemir, who was arriving from Germany, he accepted a lift in order to do some much-needed grocery shopping. Little did he suspect what entertainment he had in store.

The fact that Anton rarely, if ever, drove an empty van became immediately evident as Kevin, Anton, and four large workers piled into the seats, a capacity seating that didn't stop them from picking up an elderly woman a hundred yards down the road. Walking with a girlish gait that belied her age, she carried a heavy wicker basket, walking the four miles each way from Port Howe to do grounds work at the few seasonal homes. Next came an octogenarian, her clothes an assortment of rags. Clearly returning from a foraging expedition, she carried a basket of dried pigeon peas, the national staple, plus fistfuls of dried leaves stuffed down the bosom of her dress.

What room was vacated by departing passengers was next quickly filled by a large middle-aged couple, their two huge baskets of what looked like pumpkins, and their two dogs, one of which promptly peed in the van. Unperturbed, Anton drove on, dispensing passengers along with his quiet brand of understated wit. Anton asked why the couple didn't get a cart for their donkey, since it would make their travels to and from their assorted crops so much easier. The man replied that he had thought of that himself, and was only waiting for a man to find some wheels for him. He had been waiting for years.

Arriving at the airport, they were met by not only Waldemir, but also his wife Anna, Ludwig and Veronika, who were friends from Germany, and Waldemir's personal SCUBA diving expert (who we promptly dubbed The Dive King). The previous passenger count seemed like child's play as they now squeezed in seven amply-endowed adults, a generous quantity of luggage, abundant SCUBA gear, and two large boxes of groceries. Waving Anton aside, Waldemir took the wheel, flying off in a cloud of dust.

"Ah, Waldemir," Anton remarked as Waldemir handled the road like he was cruising the German autobahn, "you might want to slow down up ahead."

"What's that?" Waldemir shot back, barely evading one of the many gaping potholes.

"The oil pan is leaking," continued Anton. "You might want to slow down."

"Yes, yes," Waldemir replied with enthusiasm, showing no signs of doing any such thing. Suddenly he bottomed out on a pothole, sending both vehicle and passengers into a vibrating spasm. "I must have been away longer than I thought," he grinned. "I used to know where all the potholes were."

Clearly, Waldemir was enjoying himself, potholes, leaky oil pan, cramped quarters, and all. General bonhomie was at an all time high as Waldemir suddenly veered off down a dirt road.

"We must stop at the Pilot House for something to drink," he exclaimed. Drinking, to a German, meant beer and Kevin, having seen the Pilot House advertised in various tourist guides, was all for the detour. Careening down the road, oblivious to a probably rapidly-deteriorating oil supply, he pulled to a halt in front of the small restaurant. Three women and a child sat quietly on the front porch, the only apparent sign of activity.

"Are you open?" Waldemir bellowed.

"Yes," one of them drawled, "We're open."

Open is a loosely applied term in the Bahamas, rather like "I'll be around." While "around" can mean anywhere on the island, "open" simply means you can get in the door. What you might find there is anyone's guess. In this case, due to a broken cooler, the count amounted to some wine and one cold beer that had been stored in the freezer. In fact, it was so cold it was frozen. Undaunted, Waldemir fetched glasses, opened warm beers, then proceeded to mix the warm with the rapidly thawing frozen one. Everyone was soon knocking back thimble-fulls of tepid beer, watching a spectacular sunset from the Pilot House deck and being vastly entertained by Waldemir's ribald remarks exchanged with the three laughing ladies.

Nor did things slow down as the evening wore on. From beer at the Pilot House, Waldemir progressed through rounds of courtesy drinks at the Greenwood bar, an exuberant dinner hour, and a liberal dispensing of after-dinner liqueurs. Finding ourselves meekly following his lead and dousing our desserts with cognac, we understood all too clearly how Anton and Carolyn had arrived in the guise of guests and found themselves suddenly running the place.

* * * *

Mailboat Delivery

Among the Out Islands, the mailboat delivery is an integral part of island life, serving as the primary supply link. Without it, little mail or goods would arrive. With it, each island manages to keep at least a tenuous link with the rest of the country, or in the case of the southern islands, the dominating force of Nassau. Mailboat day is the pivotal day of the week, with people rushing to buy the newly arrived goods while they last. The mailboats themselves are as varied as the islands, in appearance, punctuality, efficiency and friendliness. Rated on a scale from one to ten, Cat Island's mailboat would hit rock bottom. Arriving each Wednesday from Nassau, it docks at the government wharf in New Bight, thus beginning a weekly ritual that left a lasting impression on Kevin and the boys.

Accepting the invitation to accompany Anton, they set off for what was clearly going to be the morning's entertainment. We had encountered Out Island mailboats before, riding the one between Spanish Wells and Harbour Island years ago when the children were only four. The Cat Island boat, however, was a different breed all together, ruled by a crew that regarded organization as an alien concept. As Carolyn said, if she got half of what she ordered, she was lucky.

Tied up alongside the dock, the boat began disgorging quantities of goods from its hold, depositing them on the wharf in a haphazard fashion. The challenge lay in finding what you had ordered, or even if it had arrived, no easy task when you considered that everyone else was doing exactly the same thing. Everything for the Greenwood Inn was supposed to be packaged together and labeled as such. In fact, the deckhand in charge insisted it had been loaded that way in Nassau. "I saw it with my own eyes, man," he assured them, repeating an obviously well-worn phrase. Yes, it was quite a miracle, Anton remarked, the way those goods mixed themselves up on the way to Cat Island each week. In the end, it took them two hours to track down all the errant cases of food, an ordeal that left Tristan and Colin breathless. Never again, they vowed, would they complain about grocery shopping. The idea of undertaking this on a weekly basis was mind-boggling. Anton, as always, accepted it with the equanimity that enabled him to cope with all aspects of rural island life.

* * * *

Walks

Remote and sparsely populated, Cat Island offers some lovely places to walk. The predominant feeling is of a lush landscape compared to Great Exuma and Long Island, of gently rolling land that rises in places to recognizable hills, including Mt. Alvernia, the highest point in the Bahamas. We discovered a number of walks, exploring the countryside around the Greenwood Inn. Most led from the inn down a series of dirt roads, ostensibly part of the planned one-thousand-home development. The vegetation was varied, sprinkled with colorful wildflowers, the views often perfect out across the treetops to the brilliant blue water. A beach lay hidden below, only hinted at by sudden flashes of white sand through narrow, bush-lined footpaths.

One side road turned uphill, passing a couple of homes tucked into the landscape, then dropping away to a fine view across a long, shallow lake filled with the sound of birds. Birds are abundant on Cat, attracted by the many brackish lakes and undisturbed natural habitats. Most keep well hidden in the undergrowth, dashing quickly across the road in a tantalizing flash of turquoise or sea green. One small pond, a five minute walk from the inn, is known for its birdlife, best visited at dawn or dusk when sightings are most common.

Perhaps most popular of all is a walk along the beach, following the line of coast both north and south of the inn. A sand dune lines the shore, topped by thick bushes, clusters of coconut palms, and delicate flowers. One highly recommended route is an hour walk south to Honeymoon Beach, a crescent of sand nestled between two rocky points that can only be reached on foot and at low tide.

Venturing farther afield, there are equally lovely places to walk in the interior, or along the western shore, whether exploring a scenic village like Port Howe, climbing Mt. Alvernia, or venturing into a hidden Blue Hole. Explored on foot, Cat Island is truly a naturalist's, outdoor-lover's delight.

* * * *

Deveaux Mansion

Like much of what happens at the Greenwood Inn, the opportunity to visit the historic Deveaux Mansion evolved out of a need to shuttle workers to and from the inn. At Carolyn's suggestion, Kevin provided transport home for the morning shift of girls so we could stop off and see the mansion on our way back. Lying beside the village school in Port Howe, the crumbling mansion remains the best preserved of the Out Islands' once plentiful plantation homes. As usual, a Cat Island outing provided a mixture of natural beauty, historic import, and social insight. Piled into the van with the four girls, we headed for Port Howe, Bain Town and Zonicles, three small villages strung along the coastal route that meanders around the southern tip of Cat. First stop was Port Howe, home of Sheila, a plump, friendly young woman who quickly ingratiated herself to me by whisking off Gwyneth's dirty diapers to launder. Possessed of a ready laugh, she relished my story of the disappearing diapers on Long Island. Later she would proudly show me her own baby's cloth diapers, explaining she had received them from a friend in the States. Cloth diapers and rubber pants are coveted items in these islands, where only disposables are available, always at exorbitant cost. This paradox of Third World living standards coupled with the prevalence of high-cost disposable products is something we continue to see throughout our travels, suggesting that some large companies are doing an unethical marketing job in the wrong quarter.

In Zonicles, we were supposed to pick up a girl named Delrey, a process that involved yet again that characteristic Bahamian quirk for precision that we'd first encountered with the Exuma taxi. Having initially missed our turn into Zonicles, a situation that reduced the remaining girls to a fit of giggles, we drove past a number of simple homes before being directed up a rough, dirt road. As the road was little more than a track going almost vertically uphill, Kevin pulled to a stop. A small house stood to the left in a grove of trees, another somehow perched atop the steep hill. "Keep going," the girls insisted. "You ain't there yet. We'll tell you when to stop." Kevin and I looked at each other. Even Waldemir, we were willing to bet, wouldn't attempt that hill in the van. Still, they were acting pretty insistent, urging Kevin on impatiently. Exhibiting every sign of reluctance, Kevin eased off the brake and inched forward a car's length. "Stop right there!" they cried.

Delrey turned out to be a cute fifteen-year-old whom Carolyn and Anton had befriended through her occasional work in the Greenwood kitchen. Taking her under their wing, they were attempting to wean her away from evenings spent at the local bar and the prospect of a common fate for island girls—a teenage pregnancy—by providing her with a place to come and do her homework in the evening. With no electricity and primitive conditions at home, there was little incentive for her to stay there. As always, it amazed us how clean and tidy women and children were when emerging from the most basic of living quarters. Dressed in a white blouse, dark skirt and dress-up shoes, Delrey appeared looking ready for a party, a reflection of the importance an evening at the Greenwood held for her.

Back in Port Howe, we parked beside the shuttered schoolhouse, climbing out to explore the Deveaux Mansion. Despite one hundred years of neglect, much of the place is still intact. Sturdy stone walls, solid ceiling and floor beams, and shingled roof bare testimony to an earlier glory. The ruins include the accompanying bake house, with its towering chimney and long, rectangular slave quarters. Built within a stone's throw of the main house, the close presence of the slave quarters is a telling sign of the interdependence that prevailed in the Bahamas between plantation owner and slave, a far cry from the social chasm that existed between the two in the southern United States. This same affinity led many departing plantation owners to leave their property, as well as their name, to their freed slaves, thus setting the stage for a freedom from racial tensions that the country enjoys today.

Despite her tight skirt and delicate party shoes, Delrey disappeared suddenly, reappearing on the upper story of the ruin as if by magic. As with all local children from the neighboring primary school who regarded the mansion as an extension of their playground, she'd rapidly learned how to scale the wall and haul herself up through what was once a stairwell. Judging from the ten-foot high ceiling, gaping hole, and worn rock wall, this was no mean feat. Aided by her directions, Tristan and Colin soon found the hidden toeholds and followed suit.

The mansion was well worth the visit, its forlorn grandeur a reminder of a previous affluent age. The plantation era was doomed from the beginning in the Out Islands, for the thin topsoil and lack of water made the growing of sugarcane impractical compared to the Caribbean islands farther south.

* * * *

Greenwood Social Life

The Greenwood, similar to a number of Out Island resorts, is one of those places where a dinner-hour social life prevails. Built on a small scale and cultivating an aura of intimacy, it quickly breaks down the barriers imposed by strangers thrown together in close proximity. Coupled with Waldemir's imposing presence and Carolyn and Anton's Midwestern brand of friendliness, it's the rare guest that can resist the appeal of such entertaining mingling. The bar, merely an extension of the diningroom, serves as a place for guests to congregate before dinner. Accompanied by Gwyneth, I usually found myself seated in one of the large armchairs while the baby clung to a low coffee table in her efforts to stand up. A series of people seemed to periodically occupy the chair adjacent, rather like a well orchestrated version of musical chairs, the object here being to keep the conversation flowing.

The guests were a varied lot on any given night. Carolyn made periodic visits to the chair to keep me abreast of new arrivals, doling out a quick appraisal with her customary humor. Tristan and Colin, practically bribed into substituting khaki pants for shorts, soon discovered the ring game, a prevalent bar game that involves nothing more than attempting to hook a ring suspended from a string over a hook mounted on the wall. Simple, but endlessly entertaining, given the level of competition imposed by the Bahamian work force that frequently ended their days with a brief interval at the bar. Next, there was always Waldemir and his entourage: Anna, Waldemir's wife, invariably clothed in flowing pieces of material that passed for a dress, exuding an air of fragility as she alighted periodically in the chair for a chat about such topics as adventure travel writing and her artistic pursuits; Ludwig, round-faced and comical, who vacillated between discussing classical composers to the state of a reunified Germany.

Diana and Pamela, two divorced mothers vacationing together, were a study in contrasts. Pamela, dark, thin and classically pretty, savored her vacation from a spot in the sun, spending hours on the beach with a novel in hand. Diana, her wildly-curly hair tumbling down her back, exuded pure energy, pursuing with devotion the esoteric pleasures of fly-fishing. As she told me confidentially, few Bahamians would understand the business of fly fishing, where the pleasure is all in the challenge, not the result, and fish are usually put back. What satisfaction there is comes later in the story telling. Bahamians, on the other hand, take it as a matter of pride to return from any fishing expedition loaded with seafood. Later she would meet the quintessential local fisherman, who possessed both the Bahamian's infallible ability at harvesting food with the purist's pursuit of catch-and-release.

Peter and Moni were on a twenty-four hour visit to view the property of a friend. Fresh from New York City, they exuded a combination of moneyed elegance and childlike wonder that such places as Cat Island exist. Peter, a real estate investor, was just that conservative, "pretty" sort that teenage girls lust after, while Moni, a Russian model, possessed the kind of leggy good looks that strikes envy into every woman's heart. Conversation with them soon bogged down in the superlative, with them thinking we led the life of ultimate glamour— writing, travel, the tropics and all that, although I doubt they would care for living on our income. If there's one thing we've learned, falling as we do in the so-called "fantasy life-style" bracket, it's that there is no such thing as the perfect life-style. All have their drawbacks and require sacrifices: Royalty sacrifice privacy and the right to live their own lives; the famous sacrifice privacy and peace of mind; the rich often sacrifice a goal in life; creative people sacrifice security; and the retired have often sacrificed their youth. The best we can aspire to is to be able to look back and honestly say that we lived life to the fullest.

Nearby residents frequently arrived for dinner, one of whom button-holed Kevin in the bar one night. A belligerent type who specialized in offensive remarks, he launched the conversation with a startling "Cat Island isn't a place for young people."

"Oh really? Why's that?" Kevin replied with re-strained politeness.

"Well, there's no casinos and things. You wouldn't like it here."

One got the impression that his message was that he wouldn't like young people here, that he loathed the youth of the world and had moved all the way to Cat Island just to escape them.

Occasionally, boaters showed up, ferried in the ubiquitous van from the anchorage at New Bight. One memorable evening included two couples off sailboats cruising tandem. One young woman, a garrulous, vivacious girl from New York City, didn't hide the fact that cruising to her was best enjoyed as a series of anchorages. Letting her Russian boyfriend do the passages single-handed, she flew down to join him at periodic desirable stops, thus enjoying the pleasures of sailing with few of the discomforts. Unequal to the task of reorienting her urban tastes, she found the thought of dining out infinitely preferable to coping with the limitations of a galley, even if the restaurant was half an hour's drive away.

Presiding over all this social diversity was the staff: Carolyn and Anton, looking calm and organized; the waitress Dannie Mae in her bright yellow print dress; and Eula, the lovely teenage bartender, a role she had assumed one evening in the absence of anyone more qualified. As Waldemir's idea of procuring a drink was to make it himself, he didn't care if her talents were more visual than practical, although she was fast learning to produce a credible mixed drink. The atmosphere was invariably friendly and convivial, almost like that of a family thrown together for a holiday, with everyone catching up on past news. Sometimes we dined together at a long, central table, sometimes separated into smaller, more intimate groups. The food was delicious, featuring the abundance of fresh seafood and Carolyn's flair for desserts.

* * * *

Mount Alvernia

At a mere 207 feet, Mt. Alvernia on southern Cat
Isand is the tallest point in the Bahamas. Topped by The
Hermitage, the religious retreat of a mid-twentieth
century hermit, it offers one of the most fascinating
sights in the Out Islands. Eager to share the beauties of
their island with guests, Carolyn and Anton drove us
there, as it lies only ten miles from the Greenwood. The
ride supplied the usual diversions, principally being
momentarily stopped by the police, who were busy
trying to explain how it was they happened to smash up
the van, and why they should pay the damages. Their
original story of being forced off the road was starting to
look a bit thin in the absence of any culprit and their
eagerness to complete the matter at their cost.

Once off the main road, a rough track led through the
ruin of a house (the children were vastly amused as
Anton drove right through the front door) and up to the
base of the mountain. From there we walked, beginning
at the stone arch built over the entrance of the path.
Winding up through a tall, dense stand of trees, the path
climbed steeply, often becoming a series of steps cut
from the rock. Some enterprising farmer had planted the
steep hillside beside the track with corn, peas and
squash, a classic example of Bahamian agricultural
practices. Instead of removing rocks from a cultivated
garden plot, they simply plant around them. Given all
the flat ground in the vicinity, it seemed amazing that
someone had gone to the trouble of cultivating such an
inaccessible spot.

Along the path were a series of stone plaques, called
stations of the cross, cut into the rock and depicting the
various stages of Jesus carrying the cross to crucifixion.
At the top was the largest, a cave with the stone signifi-

cantly rolled aside. The land fell away abruptly on all sides, leaving a stunning view across the island in all directions and out towards the water, a spectacular effect in an otherwise low-lying country. The Hermitage, built during the 1950s by Father Jerome, the architect of numerous Bahamian churches, is truly a lovely grouping of structures, very impressive on it hilltop setting. From below, it appears at first to be a large structure on a sizeable mountain, so exact is the scale and proportion in relation to the surroundings. The chapel is square with a traditional peaked roof topped by a cross. Beside it to one side stands the belltower, tall and pointed like a minaret, to the left perhaps the most unusual building of all, his study with its flat cornered roof topped by a dome. The three buildings look almost like a religious composite of mosque, church and minaret. Father Jerome may have been first and foremost a religious hermit, but he was also a true architect.

The return trip involved yet another colorful hitch-hiker, this time a young man on his way home from what was clearly an afternoon's dubious activity. Opening the back door of the van, he fell rather than climbed into the backseat, a goofy grin beaming from his face.

"Hey, man, how you all doin'?" he breathed at us, the alcohol fumes fairly knocking us flat. "Man, it's a great day, dat for sure, man."

"You been working?" Anton asked, his humor dry as always.

"Yeah, man. I bin workin' two, maybe three hours. I tired, man, dat for sure."

"Tired?" replied Anton, "after two hours of work?"

"Sure, man. Dat plenty of work."

"What's made you tired was visiting a few bars."

The young man giggled like a toddler caught in the act.

"Yeah, man, my friends and me, we been drinkin'

some firewater." No one was going to argue that fact. Pulling to a stop in Old Bight, Anton let him out before taking the route to the Greenwood.

"Well, you've only got three more bars to get past before you're home," was his parting, laconic remark.

The young man shot us an aromatic giggle. "No, man. I drink enough today."

* * * *

Blue Hole Morning

Blue holes, deep, circular holes of one hundred feet or more, dot the interior of many of the Out Islands. Their name is derived from their brilliant color, a reflection of the sky.

Once again, Anton organized an early morning outing, involving first a stop at a handsome house in Port Howe, home of Harrison King. A vigorous man in his forties, he belied the laid-back work ethic that prevails throughout the male population of the Out Islands, combining his talents as policeman, preacher, goat herder, and occasional blue hole guide. Driving to Zonicles Hill, we piled into his beat-up truck (the back was literally wired together), with Anton, Tristan, Colin and me in the back, and Harrison, Kevin and Gwyneth Islay up front. Next came a painful half-mile up a rocky track that defied imagination when experienced from the back of a pick-up. The fact that we were driving was absurd. A child could have walked faster. No wonder his truck was in bad shape. If we kept this up, I thought, we'd soon follow suit.

It was all I could do to maintain my precarious seat on the wheel well, while the noise was deafening as the bits of wired-together metal bounced around under the impact. The track led back to a huge, shallow lake, whipped up to a muddy brown by the day's high winds. Although Cat Island has many inland lakes, all are brackish, and fresh water is a precious commodity. Stopping at a wire fence, we took to walking (thank God), following the fence deeper into the scrub growth. Harrison stopped to show us a number of edible plants, a food source settlers once relied on. Goats, used only for their meat in the Bahamas, could be heard foraging through the dense undergrowth, part of Harrison's herd of twenty-five.

The final route deviated down a narrow goat path where the blue hole appeared as if by magic. Despite overcast skies, the sight was impressive, an almost perfect circle cut from the land. Underwater, an emerald green ledge was clearly visible, dropping off suddenly into the near blackness of a one hundred foot depth. Small pools of water dotted the perimeter, evidence of the tidal effect that proves many of these holes are fed from the sea. Mussel-like shellfish clung to rocks under the surface, while tiny fish swam about feeding. As no large fish are found there, the access from the sea must be small. So far, no diver has found it, despite numerous attempts. The effect was impressive, especially coming on the heels of our trip to Mt. Alvernia. Within twenty-four hours we had seen both the highest and one of the lowest points in the Bahamas.

* * * *

Basketball Sunday

Basketball Sunday loomed up, the day some of the local Port Howe youths had accepted a challenge from Kevin. Having dropped off the morning shift of workers on our way in the van, we arrived at Sheila's house, a bright green affair with oceans of laundry hanging on a backyard clothesline. Outside stood not only the one basketball hoop in town, but assorted parked cars, the ice cream van, and numerous Bahamians shooting hoops, not to mention a plethora of women and girls. The Cat Islanders were obviously ready to take on the white boys. Among the players were Sheila's tall, string-bean of a teenage brother and her short, muscular, fourteen-year-old son Julian. We had encountered Julian before, at the Greenwood Inn where he managed to make a whole day's work of sweeping the front walk and pool area. Seemingly bereft of energy at the time, once on the basketball court he couldn't be stopped.

While the basketball game got underway, I wandered inside Sheila's house, one of the best built and outfitted in Port Howe. It turned out the house actually belonged to her mother, and like many southern Out Island homes, was full of women and children. Sheila, her mother, various sisters, and numerous children all lived there. Few couples marry, with most children born illegitimate and many men keeping more than one "wife", making Clifford Dean's musical mates quite socially acceptable. This also explains why so many women work. Their faith in the loyalty and security of their men is practically non-existent. Families value girl children most, with every woman wishing for a daughter. As Sheila put it, "Boy babies grow up and make trouble, but girl babies grow up and take care of you."

Once we were inside, the entire interior was practically visible at a glance; kitchen area to the right, livingroom on the left, and a few bedrooms hinted at to the rear. The front door had a screen, the windows louvered shutters, signs of prosperity. Carpets covered the floor and couches sat on either side of a low coffee table. In one corner stood two television sets and a VCR, for which they had three home movies, courtesy of an American friend. The selection, prominently displayed on a shelf, was almost a composite of film types: Sister Act (providing comedy), Aladdin (the cartoon), and The Secret Garden (for the cerebral). A Swedish Ivy graced the center of the coffee table, photographs hung on the walls, and one corner was dominated by a giant turtle shell.

An elderly, vacant-eyed man sat on a stool by the kitchen counter, while Sheila comfortably occupied one couch, her ten-month-old daughter Felicia in her lap and a rambunctious three-year-old Julius bouncing off the walls. Most attentive to Gwyneth was a lovely little girl of about eight named Celia, the daughter of Sheila's friend. As other women and girls wandered in and out, I found it impossible to sort out family origins. I got the feeling that anyone's home was open to whoever happened to be passing by, and the need for privacy unheard of. As usual, Gwyneth was an instant success, particularly her blue eyes and blonde hair, a never-ending source of delight to dark-skinned peoples. There's nothing quite like having a baby to pave the way into a foreign society. Gwyneth immediately felt at home in all this solicitous, female company, clamoring about and screeching loudly as Celia trotted out a host of stuffed animals and dolls for her entertainment. With all the floors carpeted, I could finally relax and not worry about her falling flat on her face, although she quickly zeroed in on the Swedish Ivy centerpiece with the single-minded persistence of all infants. I hadn't been there five minutes before the contrast between Gwyneth's and Felicia's behavior hit me between the eyes. While Gwyneth Islay acted like a baby Olympian in training, Felicia sat immobile on Sheila's lap, finger in mouth, eyes watching with fascination. Large for her age, she presented a comical figure, with her enormous, batwing ears, long face, hair dressed in tiny braids sticking straight out from her head, and sudden smile, dominated by two enormous front teeth. Gwyneth could have learned a lot from her about sitting sedately in laps without pawing people to death.

Sheila proudly showed me everything: Felicia's cloth diapers and rubber pants, specially delivered from Miami; her selection of videos and family photos; her small hair-dressing business next door to the house (complete with a cot so she could snatch some moments alone for herself). It came to me as I was visiting that what made this so much more interesting than other foreign encounters in private homes was the ease with which we could communicate. Without fluency in a shared language, conversations can never progress past the mundane.

Gwyneth finally started getting restless about the time Sheila decided to play excerpts from Sister Act, an experience I wasn't sure even politeness could get me through. Loading the baby into her Snugli, I headed outside where I noticed that what had begun as a very serious competition had progressed into the locals giving Kevin and the boys high fives. A positive sign, I assumed. Sure enough, the next morning Sheila arrived with the telling news. Judgement, she informed us, had been passed the previous evening following the game. "Them white guys," was the verdict, "can sure play some ball."

* * * *

Eleuthera

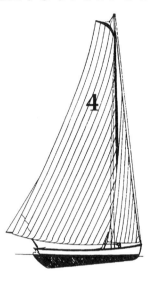

Long and lush, Eleuthera is the "garden" island of the Bahamas, with its fields of bananas and citrus, its aura of industriousness. Coming from the south, we found the pace faster, the roads better, the cars more plentiful, the people more sophisticated. This is an island for those who like more familiar territory, a cross between Bahamian charm and twentieth-century progress.

The Arrival

Tom Jones was waiting at the New Bight airport when we arrived, smiling beside his comfortably-large looking, twin-engine plane. An entrepreneur of some local repute, Tom maintained a number of successful business ventures while shuttling between his home in Georgia and house on North Eleuthera. Kevin knew him through business connections, working for the company that sold him a complete photovoltaic solar system for his Bahamas house a few years ago.

Climbing into the six-seater, I felt more confident. The plane had two engines, Kevin knew the pilot and an official-looking name graced the side of the aircraft, advertising Tom's popular *The Pilot's Guide to the Bahamas and Caribbean* (Pilot Publications). The whole business exuded a comfortable air of reliability.

Settled in my backseat, I waited for the brief speech concerning safety features, the preliminary warming of engines, the gentle taxiing down the runway. I waited in vain. Fairly leaping into the pilot's seat, Tom threw the aircraft into gear, zipped down the runway at a brisk clip, took the corner on what felt like one wheel, and was off. Once in the air, he handled the plane like a sports car—one hand on the wheel, eyes on Kevin, while keeping up a running commentary. In the aftermath, the general feeling was of having been shot by cannon from one island to another.

Coming from Cat, stepping out at Eleuthera was like re-entering the twentieth century. The recognizable airport, complete with terminal and staff, teamed with activity, including the loading of a large jet destined for Canada. We'd already seen more people than during our entire stay on Cat.

Gwyneth threw a slight delay into the taxi proceedings by needing an obvious diaper change, a fact I discovered when the back of my dress became noticeably damp from her perch in the baby backpack. "No problem," David, our taxi driver, assured us with unflappable Bahamian charm. "If they can't do it for themselves, you've got to."

Loaded up and off, we discovered that Eleuthera taxis, despite a slight improvement in appearance, possessed the same proclivity for defective exhaust systems. Everyone rolled down windows and gasped for air as the car sped down the smooth road towards Governor's Harbour. "That too much wind back there?" David asked. No, we assured him, it wasn't.

The taxi driver, as always, was accommodating to our needs. Stop number one was the Governor's Harbour grocery store, an impressive structure that promised great things, but turned out to have the usual limited selection once inside. The bakery, stop number two, was a thriving business located down a side street. Dashing inside for some loaves of bread, Kevin emerged with treats for everyone, including David. By now David practically felt like one of the family as he followed us into the grocery store, shared in our bakery purchases, dispensed advice, made recommendations, and generally kept the conversation rolling as only a Bahamian can. Talking with him, you felt, as with most Bahamians, that his friendliness was sincere, his questions not merely a polite gesture, but a reflection of genuine interest.

Unique Village, our destination, proved to be far superior to its trite name. Our villa was lovely, beautifully located on a high bluff overlooking a private stretch of beach and the ocean. Our stay there was to be lovely and peaceful, the view and attendant beach irresistible. The timing couldn't have been better, for the whole alluring package helped lessen the effect of having left Cat. Eleuthera, we knew, wouldn't offer the intensity of our experience on Cat Island, but its tropical beauty, its comfortable accommodations, interesting sights, and attractive beaches would prove ample compensation.

*　　*　　*　　*

Island Travel

Going places, we soon discovered, seemed to be a favored Eleuthera pastime, perhaps because of its size, ease of travel and sizeable North American population. Whatever the reason, driving places in a car seemed to be a popular daily option. Unlike the other Out Islands we had visited, Eleuthera supplies an infrastructure that supports ease of travel by car: good roads, plentiful rental cars (some in better shape than others), numerous restaurants and shops, places to stay, and a variety of island activities and scenic sites. Seasonal residents, capitalizing on these benefits, have brought with them the penchant for mobility that one finds in affluent, urban cultures. After the near non-existent transport on Cat Island, the bicycles and resort pick-up on Long, the infrequent modes of transport on Exuma, one day spent at Unique Village seemed like a return to suburbia. With only three villas, it didn't take long to meet our neighbors on both sides, two couples from Massachusetts on their yearly retreats to the quieter life-style of the Bahamas. They both had smart-looking vehicles and it seemed they were always driving off in pursuit of food, secluded beaches and island points of interest. Nor were they alone in making the most of their vehicles. Friends arrived almost hourly, with what seemed like a never-ending supply of invitations to happenings on the island. Despite Eleuthera's large size by Bahamas standards, no one seemed to think twice about a quick excursion to the other end of the island. Not only did they have cars, but good cars, the kind they must have practically hand delivered to the island themselves to receive them in that condition. Many tourists we met also enjoyed car travel. It is an excellent way to see the entire island, but you must take care not to miss truly experiencing its slow, seductive tempo.

* * * *

Walks & Neighbors

Indulging my usual passion for explorations on foot, I set off one morning with a sleeping baby on my back, choosing the dirt lane that wound past Unique Village. Narrow and shaded by tall pines, it passed a shallow lake dotted with graceful egrets and a single blue heron, past a number of imposing drives to what were undoubtedly equally impressive homes, then out along the coast where tiny pockets of sand lay tucked along the predominantly rocky shore. The entire area seemed to be an enclave of foreigners, their attendant "No Trespassing" and "Private Property" signs a jarring note amidst the friendly hospitality of the Bahamians.

Another walk took us across the island to South Palmetto Point, not, unfortunately, an interesting route due to the rather dull scenery and numerous cars. We passed an excellent grocery store, then met an entertaining couple fresh from England who were visiting their son, a teacher in the local school. We also had a chance encounter with a young man selling guavas, a fruit we made valiant efforts to eat in its natural state before deciding it was best enjoyed in the form of jelly. Having discovered a noticeable lack of fresh produce in the local stores, we learned that the best way to buy it was to chase down a van which, with typical Bahamian flair for the unorthodox, had the word Bakery painted on the side.

In between walks, grocery shopping, and excursions to the beach, we got to know our neighbors and their

Unique Village, North Palmetto Point

Reservations:	809-332-1830
Direct Phone:	809-332-1830
Direct Fax:	809-332-1838

Location: Just south of Governor's Harbour on the ocean side of Eleuthera.

Accommodations: (3) 2-bedroom villas with kitchens and a small hotel with (4) superior double rooms (lower level) and (4) deluxe double rooms (upper level).

Getting There: Many airlines service Governor's Harbour airport on Eleuthera; take a taxi from the airport to Unique Village.

Local Transport: Rental cars and taxis.

Meals: Self-catering in the villas, or eat in the beautiful restaurant overlooking the ocean (AP, MAP, EP or by the meal); non-guests are welcome at the hotel restaurant.

Amenities: Bar and restaurant, beach towels, small beach in front of hotel, laundry service.

Phones: There is a direct line at the front desk and there are pay phones in town.

Electricity: Eleuthera has reliable utility electricity.

Water: The water in the rooms is drinkable.

Laundry: The hotel has a laundry service and there is a laundromat nearby.

Food Stores & Restaurants: Good local stores plus larger markets and restaurants in Governor's Harbour.

Highlights:

- This lovely little hotel has nice rooms and three attendant villas overlooking the Atlantic.

- The setting is extremely private and quiet.

- The rooms and villas are clean and well-appointed.

- The beachfront location offers great ocean views.

- There is privacy yet close proximity to shopping and activities in Governor's Harbour.

- The restaurant and bar area is attractive and offers a magnificent view of the ocean.

- There is a good walking road to the south with few cars and pleasant scenery.

- The hotel is centrally located for exploring both ends of the island.

friends, all of whom appeared to be from New England. Initially, it was a bit unnerving to discover we'd traveled this far only to find ourselves surrounded by the same kind of people we'd left at home. I kept expecting my parents to pop in any moment, not the usual state of affairs during our foreign travels. Everyone seemed to be dripping with money: yachts and homes in the States, winter retreats on Eleuthera, and trips abroad to fill in the gaps. Despite our different focus and financial bracket, and our book research activities ("Don't tell anyone about this place!" was the classic response), everyone was friendly and welcoming. Upon hearing we were headed for the Cove Eleuthera, a resort to the north, invitations were extended for rides in their cars, as everyone seemed to be going there the same day for the annual craft fair.

* * * *

Eleuthera Beaches

Eleuthera beaches provide an element of surprise— wonderful stretches of sand tucked among the jagged rocks and cliffs that line much of the Atlantic shore. Discovering them is half the fun, as each seems special because of its unexpectedness. Our own introduction was the small beach at Unique Village, reached via a steep staircase plunging down the bluff from our porch. Tristan and Colin built a pirate fort with boards on the beach, complete with palm-trunk cannon and coconut cannon balls. There was no shortage of empty drinking bottles, either, for those drunken brawls they like to act out so much. Some passing cruise ship must have deep-sixed a whole case. Gwyneth, stripped naked except for her sunhat, served as their immodest hostage.

Later, we were shown other beaches by island residents. The hidden ones on the Atlantic, reached by footpath and tucked almost out of sight under the cliffs—these are the beaches popular with surfers, where winter winds provide the perfect wave. The long stretch of white sand at Gauldings Cay Beach is ideal for families and beginner snorkelers. Most impressive of all is the undeveloped north coast, lined with miles of sand that draws those few who sacrifice the convenience of easy access for the allure of unblemished beauty. Everywhere we went offered some patch of sand, a place to swim, waves to surf, or reefs to explore. As always, the Atlantic side is subject to the vagaries of weather, while the Caribbean side is almost always ideal for young children.

* * * *

More Island Travel

Departing from Unique Village roused more than the usual rumblings of regret. The boys didn't want to leave their fort, and none of us was ready to leave the villa. Once again, the independence of villa living had worked its magic, wooing us with its cooking facilities, its space to move about and quality of home life. Although staying in a place like this lacked the cultural intensity of other Out Island experiences, it possessed a relaxing charm of its own.

Linking up with our neighbors for the trip up-island, we were divided between the two cars. Maintaining a conversation in our car proved to be no problem. All Tristan and I had to do was listen. Connie, the wife, loved to talk, keeping up an entertaining stream of local knowledge, family anecdotes, and unexpectedly liberal viewpoints. Spurred on by Connie, her quiet, unobtrusive husband turned the forty-five minute trip into a sight-seeing tour, taking in many of the local points of interest along the way. A detour through the old part of Governor's Harbour passed lovely, wooden houses trimmed with gingerbread, with their white walls and pastel trim. Tiny gardens, ornate woodwork and narrow, twisting roads typified this older side of town, built overlooking the wide, exposed harbor. Back on the main road, we continued past the airport, then deviated off onto an Atlantic coastal road, a patched and worn affair that clung to the cliff shore, passing numerous large homes owned by North Americans and Europeans. While no surf swept the shore today, it can be spectacular in an onshore tradewind, with surfers coming from afar to challenge the waves. Island vegetation began to look more barren and windswept than to the south, reminiscent of Exuma. Some of this could be attributed to the recent destruction caused by hurricane Andrew, which had raged across North Eleuthera two years earlier.

Back inland, the road continued through an area of gently rolling hills previously used for cattle ranching. All that remains are tall cement silos towering over the bleak landscape like eerie monoliths. A successful venture during colonial times, cattle ranching died out with the coming of independence, as did much of the enterprise in the Bahamas. Grandiose development schemes, like those at Stella Maris and the Greenwood also dated from that period, with investors losing faith after the country gained independence.

Farther on, we passed the dirt road entrance to some wonderful cave Connie insisted we must see. As she also mentioned it was covered with graffiti and had numerous stalagmites removed by sledgehammer, I had my doubts. It's interesting, this concept of things that must be seen by tourists. Usually overrated and overtouristed, they rarely live up to reputation in our opinion. It's the unexpected discoveries that leave a lasting impression, places enjoyed on your own and free from the trappings of the tourist trade. In all fairness, classic tourist sights in the Bahamas escape much of the commercialism and overcrowding that pervade other scenic spots, with some even retaining the magic of the newly discovered.

* * * *

Gauldings Cay Beach

With only a miniature sand beach on the premises (perfect for young children, sunbathers, hammock aficionados, and snorkelers), the Cove Eleuthera provided free morning transport to Gauldings Cay Beach, three miles down the road. Bicycling was also possible on the level, well-paved road. Anne, the vastly entertaining hotel owner, drove us in the resort vehicle, a derelict Cadillac Coup de Ville that retained only a vestige of its former glory. The condition of the car was a familiar sight after weeks of Out Island travel: ubiquitous dingy brown color so typical of Bahamian vehicles (because it blends well with the dust?), broken passenger door handle, peeling vinyl seats, missing ceiling cover, and the usual backseat exhaust system. All this, as Anne put it, for the bargain price of $2,500. Even derelict cars are expensive in the Out Islands. With the demise of her previous car, this was the best she could do on short notice until her new vehicle arrived at some indeterminate future date. Nothing happens fast in the Bahamas, especially the delivery of goods coming through the infamous Nassau bottleneck.

The Cove Eleuthera, Gregory Town

Reservations:	800-552-5960, 603-437-4155
Direct Phone:	809-335-5142
Direct Fax:	809-335-5338

Location: Just north of Gregory Town on the Caribbean side of Eleuthera.

Accommodations: There are seven dwellings dotted around the grounds, each with four double rooms. The rooms are fairly small, but comfortable.

Getting There: Many commercial airlines service North Eleuthera airport; take a taxi from the airport to The Cove Eleuthera.

Local Transport: Rental cars, taxis, and bicycles.

Meals: MAP and AP available, or by the meal; reasonable prices, with one bargain main dish at every evening meal.

Amenities: Pool, bar and restaurant, small beach behind hotel, snorkeling, 2 tennis courts, bicycle rentals, and laundry service.

Phones: There is a direct line at the front desk, and pay phones in Gregory Town.

Electricity: Eleuthera has reliable utility electricity.

Water: The water in the rooms is drinkable.

Laundry: The hotel has a laundry service.

Food Stores & Restaurants: There is a good food market, bakery and alternative restaurant in Gregory Town.

Highlights:

- The Cove Eleuthera is a small, casual resort, the kind one quickly feels at home in.

- The quiet beachfront location has great snorkeling and beautiful sunsets.

- The Caribbean side beaches are usually more tranquil than the ones on the ocean side.

- The pool area is a great place to eat, relax and watch the sunsets.

- There are two tennis courts, bicycle rentals and many local areas to explore, including some of the best surfing beaches in the Bahamas.

- The restaurant has good food at moderate prices.

Gauldings proved to be an excellent children's beach, located on the Caribbean side, with shallow water extending a long distance from shore. The warm water, absence of waves, fine sand, casuarina shade trees, and snorkeling around the nearby cay kept everyone happy. Signs of hurricane Andrew were evident in the decimated treetops and salt-burned vegetation, but the tropical climate seemed to be healing the land quickly.

The Cove Eleuthera had other diversions to offer besides the endless beach experience. While each place we'd stay seemed to feature some memorable activity, here it was tennis. Armed with courtesy rackets and balls, Tristan and Colin took to the courts practically for the duration of our stay, while Gwyneth and I savored the continual pleasures of both hotel beach and deckside pool.

* * * *

Bahamas Prices

It doesn't take long in the Bahamas to realize the only drawback to this charming country is the relatively high cost of hotels, food and local travel. The trouble is that the Bahamas operates like a developing country, while charging the prices of an affluent one. A typical Bahamian scenario, for instance, was illustrated by pizza night at the Cove Eleuthera. Scanning the menu for something inexpensive, we spotted pizza at ten dollars per person, the evening "bargain". And this was indeed a bargain, with typical dinner prices at Out Island resorts consistently in the $18 to $32 per person range. Sitting down to order, we were informed there was no pizza. Why? Because the oven was broken, and not for the first time. The last time it broke, thousands were spent getting some repairman down from Nassau. As any resort owner will tell you, it's expensive and unpredictable running a business here. That's why so many restaurants don't have a printed menu, because what they have available varies so much from day to day, not to mention minute to minute. Other characteristics that seem to change hourly include what equipment is in working order, or even whom they have on duty.

The staff at Out Island resorts can be a fairly whimsical affair, with men disappearing to "go fishing", or women coming and going depending on home responsibilities. At one point in the Greenwood Inn, Carolyn found herself without kitchen staff, not even a cook. And then there was the day Waldemir and the Dive King set out for a morning of diving only to find the help had snitched the truck, trailer and boat. Seduced by the perfect weather, they'd played hookey with the lot, returning at the end of the day with an impressive catch. Carolyn, torn between amusement and frustration, said the worker's defensive technique was to tell one manager that the other one had told them to do something, rather like children attempting to explain why they'd been caught with their hands in the cookie jar.

In keeping with all this lack of predictability, you never know what you'll find when buying food at the local markets. Here on the so-called "garden" island of Eleuthera, for instance, one village might sell loads of fresh fruit while the next might tell you the only place you can find that is in Nassau. Then you'll take a walk and see grapefruit falling off the trees for lack of picking. Inefficient island infrastructure, dependency on imported food, and the difficulties of supplying a multi-island nation keep restaurant prices steep. The Cove Eleuthera did much better than most, with a tasty, inexpensive pasta dish and moderately-priced, well-prepared seafood and meat entrees each night. If traveling as a family, one solution to the high cost of meals is to ask what's available for children. Practically all resorts serve simple meals like hamburgers, eggs and sandwiches on request. Taking advantage of these reasonably-priced selections is vastly preferable to seeing an expensive meal go untouched by a fussy child.

If you want to cut costs, skip restaurant lunches and picnic on your own store-bought items, although prices will still be higher than you're used to when grocery shopping. Traditionally inexpensive snack foods such as fruit juice, milk, cookies, cereal, snack crackers, raisins, imported fruit and peanut butter are among the most expensive items, but you'll still save money. Reasonably-priced foods found in almost every store include fresh-baked bread, cream-crackers, cheese, tinned fish, and at least some type of local produce. With children on a two-month trip, we soon found ourselves regulating their intake because of the high cost of most foods. As one of the children said in frustration one day, "Isn't there anything I can eat that I don't have to measure first?"

One good solution when on a short one- or two-week visit is to bring some time-honored high-energy kid foods like peanutbutter, nuts, raisins, rice cakes, wheat crackers, or cereal with you. Don't be embarrassed to bring an entire bagful if necessary. Boat charterers do this regularly.

*   *   *   *

Travels With Anne

Anne Mullin is one of those delightful characters who specializes in uttering outrageous statements with an element of charm. Dressed in flowing dresses, exuding boundless energy, she seems to be everywhere, one minute officiating in the office, the next joining a table for some dinner-time chat, or chauffeuring guests in the derelict Caddy. As she put it, "After a career as an elementary school teacher, I learned to be a good organizer."

Late one afternoon we accepted an invitation to see the Rainbow Inn, another small resort Anne thought would be appropriate for families. The principle problem there seemed to be one of capacity. Formally a resort with eight apartment accommodations, hurricane Andrew had reduced the number to four after sweeping away the upper stories of all the buildings. The apartments were well equipped, the grounds inviting, and the owner we spoke with welcoming.

Having visited The Rainbow, Anne digressed into numerous detours, beginning with "Hidden Beach" out on the Atlantic shore. "Suicide Beach" would be more appropriate. First you had to toddle down the rocky trail blasted out of the cliff (nothing stops the true developer), then crawl along a ledge between the cliffs, step out onto a surf-swept beach, and make a mad dash for the one dry spot under the overhang of the cliff. All that without even having made it into the water. Great for surfers, I suppose, but idiotic for mothers with small children.

Next stop was Hatchet Bay, an area we'd heard much about from fellow boaters. The anchorage, created by blasting a hole through the rock to the lake inside, is spectacular and well protected, surrounded by wooded shores on three sides. The fourth, where boaters land ashore, is not especially attractive. Perhaps it has seen better days and will again, but during our visit the area was the site of abandoned steel drums and hurricane-damaged boats. You can, however, charter a beautiful catamaran there from Charter Cats of the Bahamas.

Continuing on, we were temporarily stuck behind a school bus that was burning oil in a truly impressive fashion. Why, we wondered, are the vehicles in the Bahamas in universally bad condition—worse than any other country we've visited? One consolation to the slowed pace was that Kevin and I had a temporary respite from Anne's unnerving technique at the wheel. Driving with the exuberance that typified all her actions, she sent the Cadillac careening down the narrow roads, eyes facing anywhere except ahead, the car bouncing from shoulder to shoulder.

Our last stop was Gregory Town, its houses spilling down the steep hillside, roosters crowing, children milling about the streets, and tiny vegetable plots appearing out of the confusion. We saw the hilltop bakery, the grocery store, the straw works and new T-shirt factory, all seemingly run by the same enterprising family. Judging from the number of gardens, goats and chickens, it was obvious how many Bahamians beat the high cost of food.

Miraculously, the Cadillac held up during this assault on its fragile state, delivering us back just in time for a restorative swim and dinner. Anne, stepping from the dusty interior, emerged looking neat and refreshed as ever. Clearly, those years with school children had been good training for the rigors of Bahamas resort management.

* * * *

Quartermoon

One day, our pilot friend Tom Jones showed up, offering us the use of his North Eleuthera house, and thus supplying us with much needed accommodations prior to our departure to Harbour Island. The house was empty, he insisted, and besides, he'd like to have Kevin take a look at his solar-powered electrical system.

Our departure from the Cove Eleuthera was colorful. The elderly taxi driver who frequented the place and was going to such pains to inject a note of elegance to the proceedings blanched as Tom roared up in his pick-up. Bags and boys were loaded into the back, along with two large water containers ("Broken water pump," Tom exclaimed. Where had I heard that before?). He immediately cranked on an enormous cassette player. Thereafter, each time we flew over a pothole at Tom's habitual breakneck speed, the cassette player either stopped or started up again. In the meantime, I was seated up front with Gwyneth between Tom and Kevin, a spot I soon discovered had a serious defect. My behind ran the risk of being scalded as the exhaust, in true Bahamian fashion, shot straight up the middle of the front seat.

At Whale Point, a long, high spit of land thrusting out into the sea, we stopped off to see Tom's future house site, suicidally perched atop a dramatic surf-swept cliff. We wondered why is it that people often look at a place like this and want to build something on it, to possess it, their way of showing appreciation for its beauty. Knowing it exists should, somehow, be good enough.

Beyond Whale Point, the road continued straight and flat, passing one or two straggling villages, the odd house here or there, and miles and miles of citrus orchards and banana groves. This is one of the main growing regions of Eleuthera, many of the farms owned by wealthy white residents of nearby Spanish Wells and Harbour Island, land originally deeded to the families during early settlement years. Tom's house, named

Quartermoon for its curved shape, sat by itself on one of the highest hilltops, its view among the most spectacular in the Bahamas. Looking out across the sparsely-populated landscape, the distant line of shore and numerous islands, we were reminded of coastal Maine. The house itself was perfect, shaped just like a quartermoon around a patio and pool, with gardens and lawn sloping down the hillside. Inside was a large living area, two separate bedroom wings, overhead ceiling fans, and all the conveniences of home. Tom rents his house to tourists when he's not in residence. For details you can contact him by phone at 912-264-4195.

Tristan and Colin quickly befriended Quarterman, Tom's caretaker/gardener. Tall, lanky and soft-spoken, he arrived daily on his vintage bicycle to diligently tend the gardens. Despite his gentle demeanor, hints were dropped of a darker past, a shady former life that Tom had helped rescue him from. He proved a wealth of local knowledge, fascinating the boys with his gardening acumen, his ability to materialize things out of thin air, his intriguing culinary habits. Hearing that we were interested in grapefruit, he mentioned that he could probably get us "a couple", a turn of phrase that instantly produced a heaping bucketful.

Tom's other help was a local cleaning woman, a tall, thin girl who swept, scrubbed and mopped with a devotion that was almost embarrassing. The fact that she was also completely deaf kept the conversation to a minimum, as well as injecting an element of the unexpected into her routine. We learned later that her ability to clean was matched by her passion for leaving things in new places, with Tom spending the remainder of each week in a veritable treasure hunt for missing items.

Left in sole possession of Tom's house, truck, pool and hired help, we reveled in our good fortune and had a great time. Quartermoon, we decided, might spoil us for life.

* * * *

Sandflies and Such

It was at Quartermoon that we encountered our first sandflies, a minuscule biting fly that goes by a variety of names. Called midges where I come from, they are also commonly known as no-see-ums, or, as one piece of hotel literature jokingly put it, the Bahamas national bird. Most screens have little effect, as the tiny flies can fly right through them. Fortunately, their saving grace seems to be an inability to land on a moving object. Sandflies are most prevalent in inland wooded areas or around mangroves, particularly after a rain or when the winds die down. Avon Skin-So-Soft products seem to be an effective, non-toxic deterrent. We actually encountered them only in the evenings at Quartermoon, where we soon learned to shut the doors and windows to avoid an invasion. Many coastal areas and all towns seem to be free of the pests. Biting insects in general are rarely a problem in the Bahamas, particularly near the water where one usually finds a breeze. Mosquitoes can show up at dusk, but they're easily avoided. Even when traveling with a baby, we never carried or wore bug repellant during our entire trip.

* * * *

Preacher's Cave

Preacher's Cave is one of those sights featured in all the tourist guides and recommended by locals, hotel staff, and taxi drivers. That fact alone is usually enough to send us scurrying the other direction, picturing something that is overrated, overtouristed and commercially exploited. So far we had limited our exposure to scenic attractions to those on Cat Island, where the almost total lack of tourists and attendant development have allowed places like the Hermitage and Deveaux Mansion to retain their authentic surroundings. Eleuthera, with its abundant visitors and their rental cars, seemed a different matter.

Our visit to Preacher's Cave came about by accident, the result of an aborted trip to Spanish Wells. Arriving at the water taxi dock for the short ride across from North Eleuthera, we learned that it cost $5 per person each way, regardless of age. No, there were no deals, no family rate, no return discount. Nor did the small, dour boat skipper have any of the characteristic Bahamian charm. At $40 just for the privilege of walking around Spanish Wells, the trip was definitely out of our budget. Besides, we had been there before, anchored for two weeks in the snug, scenic, convivial boat anchorage.

For lack of an alternative and filled with a desire to go somewhere, we took the dirt road to Preacher's Cave, a dusty, rough affair that soon had us stopping and abandoning Tom's truck in favor of walking. We weren't in a hurry and the chance for some exercise was inviting. Orchards extended across the countryside on both sides of the road, their trees laden with ripened fruit. Sounds of sheep lured the children over a wire fence and down a narrow, red-dirt road towards other orchards. Another turn in the track revealed a handful of sheep and lambs scurrying about in a flurry of indecision between taking cover and indulging their curiosity at our appearance. Noticing a gap in the dense trees to one side of the track, we stepped in and discovered a blue hole—our own secret blue hole. Cut from the limestone rock, its water filled depths reflected the deep blue-green of the sky. Trailing branches and vines from overhanging trees brushed the surface of the water, while the underbrush camouflaged its magical presence from passing eyes. Who would expect such loveliness in this dry interior?

From there, we continued on to Preacher's Cave, a delightful surprise in its natural setting and solitude. No people, no trash, and practically no graffiti. Just a narrow trail leading to an enormous, open cave, its interior lit by natural "skylights", openings in the rock that poured in streaming sunlight and splashes of greenery from above. Preacher's Cave earned its fame and name during the early settlement years on Eleuthera. A religious sect arriving from Bermuda, know as the Eleutherians, were wrecked off the north coast on the notorious Devil's Backbone reef. Making their way ashore, they discovered this large cave, subsequently spending their first winter there. For years afterwards, religious services were held in the cave in commemoration of that first year. Today, the area remains much as it had been when it was first discovered, conjuring up images of what it must have been like to land and try to make a home there.

* * * *

Swimming With The Dolphins

A footpath opposite the cave led to a perfect beach, another one easily enjoyed in lonely splendor. The sand was the finest, the water the warmest, the waves small and gentle. Just offshore lay the Devil's Backbone, with its inside passage linking the islands of Spanish Wells and Harbour Island. It takes local knowledge to make the passage safely through this area of devastating coral reefs.

Everyone swam, picnicked, built castles in the sand. Suddenly our eyes were caught by the sight of a small Whaler cruising through the passage, a host of playful dolphins following in its wake. Tiring of the show, the boat sped off, leaving the dolphins looking for new playmates, a role our children quickly dashed into the water to fulfill. The dolphins were small and frolicsome, overcoming the boys' initial shyness. For the next half-hour they swam together, a spontaneous and extraordinary moment of intimacy between man and the wild. It was a far cry from the contrived and much-advertised "swimming with the dolphins" experience offered elsewhere, where, for a price, you could swim with dolphins in captivity, a repugnant idea at best, not only in terms of what it does to the animals, but because it fosters a false attitude towards wildlife. Zoos originally set the precedent, creating a mentality that wild animals were something you could see at will, yet an animal in captivity is no longer wild, just as places you can travel to by car are no longer wilderness areas. The delightful thing about this experience was that the animals were in control, dictating the terms of play. Despite an encounter with mankind, a pleasurable one on both sides, the dolphins retained their dignity, their freedom, their wildness. The children would never forget it.

*   *   *   *

Choosing A Place To Stay

One day I met a mother from New York City, visiting the Bahamas with her eighteen-month- and four-week-old children. Tied down with babies, and simply seeking a brief respite from the northern winter, she had wanted a guaranteed trouble-free week. Yet after arriving at her chosen resort, she was filled with discontent. As she put, "I didn't expect to be given a room that's smaller than my kitchen!" Traveling with young children, she found the room too small, the service too slow, the food too expensive. What she needed was an entire villa where she had space, cooking facilities, and a hint of luxury coupled with an element of independence.

Choosing a place sight-unseen is always a gamble. Even recommended places can be a total bomb. We once traveled two grueling days across Guatemala to what we had been assured was the perfect place for us, only to find we all hated it. Everyone's needs are different. This mother, for instance, valued space, service, convenience and reasonable price, an often unrealistic combination. Her favorite vacation spot had been at a hotel catering to honeymooners on Barbados, where the service was great, the price low, and the staff doting on her young. Yet the resort was larger, more garish and less culturally stimulating than what she found and enjoyed in the Bahamas.

When trying to select a place in advance of your trip, you're often at the mercy of the travel brochures. Selective photography makes all rooms and pools look big, all surroundings look idyllic, and the descriptive writing in the brochures doesn't tell much about what it's really like to be there. Some tourist boards and travel agents aren't much help either, with both tending to get stuck on certain places, the same as the Realtor who insists on showing you split level ranches when what you really want to see are old-fashioned farmhouses. Our experience with Cat Island was a classic example. Mention Cat to anyone and you'll invariably be asked, "Did you stay at Fernandez Bay?" Any reference to the Greenwood Inn always draws a blank. I actually thought the only place to stay on Harbour Island was the Coral Sands Hotel, because that's the only place I'd ever heard mentioned.

What really doesn't make sense is that while these well known hotels are usually nice places to stay, there are often other hotels better suited to your needs.

So what is the solution? Trial and error, to a certain extent. And price. How much you are prepared to pay usually determines the level of luxury. Or how adventurous you are. A place that seems like a dog to one person might be regarded as an exciting challenge to another. Some are better for those who like towns and nightlife, others more suited to nature lovers and solitude seekers. Families with young children often have needs entirely different from those with teenagers, as do young couples from old.

Try to get a travel agent who knows what she or he is talking about, who's actually been to the country and area you're interested in. Also, the Bahama Out Islands Promotion Board has information on over 50 properties, ranging from deluxe hotels to small inns and villas throughout all of the islands mentioned in this book. Contact them for a brochure, further information or reservations at 1-800-688-4752. Beyond that, call the manager of the resort you are interested in staying at and voice your concerns. All the places covered in this book are attractive in one way or another. While the services and rooms might be less appealing in some, their cheaper price or spectacular scenery affords compensation. If you like towns, then select a centrally-located hotel, otherwise choose something farther out. For those who want room and independence, a villa is best. Those with small children will probably prefer a beach and facilities nearby. Above all, remember that the Bahamas is a foreign country and should be valued as such. If a beach and a bit of sun are all you want, you might want to choose a domestic destination.

* * * *

Harbour Island

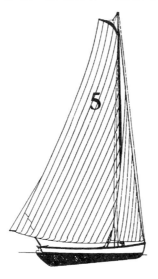

Harbour Island represents a transition point from
the developing Out Islands in the south to the industrious Abacos in the north. Settled by Royalists, populated
by blacks and whites, frequented today by the very rich,
it combines a weathered charm with worldly wealth.
Tiny boutiques and elegant restaurants, comfortable
resorts and grandiose mansions mingle with the historic
cottages of Dunmore Town, the narrow, twisting streets,
the gentle tempo of island life.

The Arrival

For the first time on our trip, getting to our next
island involved nothing more than a quick truck ride
and short ferry crossing, a seemingly tame undertaking
that still included a disproportionate amount of drama.
First, another bone-shattering trip in Tom's pick-up—
this time putting two rusty nail holes in the rear of

Tristan's shorts; then a short ferry ride across the wild, choppy harbor in a strong southerly wind. The water taxi's saving grace was a generous bimini cover that enshrouded the cockpit, as the craft sprayed water on both sides like a dual Niagara Falls and jarred our bottoms in a manner that rivaled any weight-reducing machine. Gwyneth was not thrilled, nor was my stomach. I was immensely grateful the harbor wasn't very wide.

Delivered right at the marina doorstep of Valentine's Yacht Club & Inn, we checked in and were led through lovely gardens, past a handful of small villas, and up some stairs to our wonderful room. We loved it immediately, thrilled with its spacious accommodations, twin double beds, attractive wicker and glass furnishings and excellent water view. There was even plenty of room for a crib, although no crib was yet in evidence. Nor any bath towels or trash basket. Shelving these minor needs temporarily, we headed for the pool. Best of all for travels with baby, everything was carpeted—even the pool area!

Reinforced by lunch, I trotted down to the dockside office with my list of questions and needs. Could we possibly have a crib? Oh, did we want a crib? The woman behind the desk looked obliging, but faintly surprised. Hadn't they noticed my all-too-apparent baby, the one this very moment making a valiant effort to destroy her office? Yes, they could give us bath towels and a waste basket. Complimentary beach towels? Yes, they had those right here behind the desk. After this stimulating game of twenty questions, I left.

Later we loaded up baby and daypacks and returned once more to the office to inquire where things were. The grocery store? Up one block, then down to the left...a big pink building. Bakery? The same vicinity.

Liquor store? Down a few more obscure streets, depressingly described as something you couldn't miss—we were all too familiar with those places you can't miss, guaranteed to elude even the most persistent tourist. The final irony occurred the following morning when, back at the office to inquire about a route to the beach, I was handed a complimentary map of the town, with everything conveniently shown on it.

Bahamian resorts could use some improvement in this department. Only a few offer guests a complete information sheet or introductory literature of any kind. As it's reassuring to get your bearings quickly in a new place, we continually found ourselves scrounging for facts about basic services such as beach towels and coolers, complimentary sports equipment and transport. Maybe other guests get used to it, but I always felt a bit like a bungling idiot as I tackled my inevitable list of questions.

* * * *

Dunmore Town

Dunmore Town, the one village on Harbour Island, is a lovely place, imbued with touches of New England architecture that reflect its early settlers. Stretched out along the waterfront, overlooking the large harbor that separates the island from North Eleuthera, the houses stand closely packed together. Winding, narrow lanes twist through the maze of white-clapboard homes trimmed in a variety of pastels, their cottage design reminiscent of the streets of Nantucket or Martha's Vineyard, historic New England whaling islands. Each has its own delightful touches: a tiny door leading to a hidden garden; ornate gingerbread eaves; long upper-level porches lined with latticework; white picket fences; flowers spilling everywhere; a shuttered window; nooks and crannies that lead to gates, gardens, porches, and gables. Built in the early 1800s, they reflect the wonderful architectural playfulness of that period. Now spruced up, painted and well tended, they prove as charming as they were two hundred years ago.

Facilities are plentiful, from a mundane laundromat to chic boutiques. More than any other Out Island, the atmosphere is one of seasonal affluence, of being a favored winter retreat for the rich. Golf carts ply the streets with their well-groomed drivers; shops are well stocked with expensive goods; a small, select French restaurant lies hidden behind a well tended gate. Everywhere, long-time winter residents lend the island a stylish tone. The grocery store is excellent, the bakery irresistible. There's even an ice cream shop, a tiny hole-in-the-wall affair with dutch doors, outside tables shaded by an overhanging trellis of trailing vines, and a selection of three flavors.

Here and there, more familiar elements of Bahamian culture lie interspersed amidst the chic veneer: the weekly mailboat arrival at the large, centrally located government dock; chickens clucking around the back streets; a home operated bakery with hot loaves cooling on a kitchen table; the waterfront straw market, with its long straggle of booths selling hats and baskets, handbags and dolls.

Most colorful is Cash's Liquor Store, worth a visit even for teetotalers. It sits on a quiet backstreet, a tiny, ramshackle, unpainted wood building, identified by a single sign. Venturing forth to buy a beer, we opened the door and entered the dark, crowded confines, not crowded with people, but with boxes and shelves of bottles that filled the miniature interior to bursting point.

Given the building's decrepit condition, the only thing still holding it up seemed to be the stacks of liquor cases. Customers had barely enough room for two to squeeze as far as the one long counter. Once inside, we inched our way past numerous boxes, looked around in startled appreciation, and were met by the sight of a thin woman in a faded dress who appeared to be at least a hundred years old. She eyed us silently from her precarious stance at the end of the counter. We hesitated. I mean, really...it didn't seem right to place an order for alcoholic beverage with this fragile ancient. Fortunately, at this juncture she settled the matter with a quavering "Can I help you?" This must be her, by God, Mrs. Cash in the flesh, her proprietary air obvious as she filled our order with great dignity. Armed with a single beer in its modest paper bag, we departed in a bemused state of disbelief. Returning the following evening for a repeat performance, we found her this time regally ensconced in an armchair, issuing sharp orders to a middle-aged man (probably her son) who leapt at her command. We wondered how this venerable woman got on with the rest of the neighborhood, which included a bar and poolhall to one side, Narcotics Anonymous across the street, and the very flamboyant Alcoholics Unanimous at the end of the road.

* * * *

Island Walks

Being small, Harbour Island lends itself well to being explored on foot—prowling the lovely town streets, venturing both north and south along dirt paths and narrow roads, or crossing the island, taking any one of a variety of paths or roads from Dunmore Town to the

Valentines Yacht Club & Inn, Dunmore Town

Reservations:	800-323-5655
Direct Phone:	809-333-2142
Direct Fax:	809-333-2135

Location: On the harbor side in Dunmore Town, Harbour Island.

Accommodations: There are 21 double rooms in three separate buildings.

Getting There: Many airlines service the North Eleuthera airport; take a short taxi ride from the airport to the harbour, then a water taxi directly to Valentine's dock on Harbour Island.

Local Transport: Rental golf carts and taxis.

Meals: MAP meal plan or by the meal; non-guests welcome at the bar and restaurant.

Amenities: Pool and hot tub, outdoor bar and restaurant, indoor dining area and English-style pub, dive shop, boat rentals, full service marina with space for 38 boats up to 140 ft.

Phones: There is a direct line at the front desk, and pay phones near the hotel and in town.

Electricity: Harbour Island has reliable utility electricity.

Water: The water in the rooms is drinkable.

Laundry: The hotel has a laundry service and there is a laundromat nearby.

Food Stores & Restaurants: Their are many good local food markets and bakeries, and a host of restaurants in addition to the fine dining at Valentine's.

Highlights:

- Valentine's is conveniently located in the center of Dunmore Town, one of the most attractive villages in the Bahamas.

- Despite the central location, the hotel is quiet and peaceful, built around a large area of gardens, paths, shade trees and grass.

- The rooms are large and comfortable (even for a family), with good ventilation and a balcony or terrace view of the harbor.

- The service is excellent: the daily maid service, grounds crew and dining staff.

- The pool, located beside the main dining room and pub, is large, deep and warm, with wide, easily negotiated steps; children will love it.

- Dinner is truly a gourmet affair, best enjoyed by those who appreciate good food.

- The dive shop is well equipped and can arrange a variety of diving trips.

- The marina is well protected and has excellent facilities.

famous pink sand beach on the ocean side. Here the swimming is excellent, provided a stiff east or south wind isn't blowing. Elegant homes lie sheltered in dense vegetation along the high ocean side, many of them available for rent at steep prices. Satisfying our curiosity, we poked into the other resorts—the Runaway Hill Club (very exclusive; no children, please) and Coral Sands Hotel (a thirty-three room, Florida-style hotel).

One excellent walk follows a scenic, harborside footpath to the intimate, appealing Romora Bay Club. Starting from Valentine's, we took a side street up past a large white and green-shuttered, New England-style house, then a right turn down between a group of palatial homes set in large, walled grounds. It was interesting to note that the one on the left was a land grant from George III in 1785, the one on the right a land grant from George VI in 1938. A convenient way to acquire family property, but it did make you wonder what they had done to deserve such recompense. Once down along the harbor front, the route followed a footpath under overhanging trees and skirting sweeping lawns and private estates before ending at the Romora Bay Club. The walk took about one hour at an easy pace, suitable for all ages. A third walk, the longest and in many ways the best, can only be described as The Day Of The Dobermans.

*   *   *   *

The Day of the Dobermans

We awoke with the roosters and had a bit of a giggle. Here we were in an elegant resort, complete with pool, palatial grounds, impeccable service and gourmet dining, yet roosters sounded the dawn as in any peasant domicile. Our personal resident hotel rooster seemed to be the town diehard, starting well before dawn and never quite giving up.

Heading out for another walk, we followed a dirt road from the outskirts of town to the north end of the island. This is Harbour Island's most elegant quarter, with a handful of million-dollar properties that stretch from shore to shore, their existence merely hinted at by tempting drives disappearing into the well-groomed undergrowth. One group of workmen, energetically constructing a fence beside a new estate, jokingly referred to the owner as "Lord Ashley".

The walking was easy and excellent, a situation that would have been ideal if it hadn't been for the persistent fear of encountering The Dobermans, a fear that grew with every step. Peter, the manager of Valentine's, had been the first to caution against walking the road north, warning us that there were two aggressive Dobermans with a well documented habit of rushing out and accosting people. Investigating further, we found the warning repeated by numerous residents, all of whom recommended we avoid that route entirely. Still, the walk was too tempting, the area too lovely to avoid. Feeling nonchalant at the onset, we found our nervousness increasing as we progressed down the track, each home appearing closer and closer to the road as the point of land narrowed. Gazing at scenic views and speculating about unimaginable wealth gave way to furtive glances from side to side as we approached each new property. How could we possibly relax on a walk that threatened ambush by killer Dobermans?

Finally, the suspense was too great, and catching sight of a woman carrying a child across the lawn of an elegant pink mansion, I hailed her. Did she know anything about Doberman dogs in the area, the malicious kind that specialize in molesting walkers? She laughed.

Well, there had been a Doberman once, visiting with its owner, but that was about all. The most aggressive dog on the road was an overgrown mutt of indiscriminate breeding that possessed a most cowardly nature. Relief gave way to admiration for the power of hearsay. From one visiting dog had grown a myth of intimidation involving two dogs, permanent residence, and awesome aggression. Continuing on, we arrived at the north end of the island where a magnificent view opened out across a cluster of small, uninhabited islands, the narrow harbor entrance, and the far stretches of the ocean.

* * * *

Beauty Pageant

Kicking off an intensive weekend of Easter festivities, Harbour Island hosts its annual Beauty Pageant. As the event takes place at The Reach, the marina bar/restaurant complex across from and part of Valentine's, we found ourselves attending. Signs posted around town, glossy photographs of contestants mounted at The Reach, and a horn-tooting afternoon parade laid the groundwork for what was clearly an island happening. By nine o'clock people began showing up, the men rushing for the bar, the women in tight silky outfits, dangling jewelry, spiked heels and hair piled high. Like Latin women, Bahamian blacks love to dress up, a lost art in many other modern cultures. Admission was twenty dollars, not to mention what you would spend at the bar once you were in the door. The local women paid it without question, eager to make an impressive entrance, while many of the men seemed inclined to sneak in via the docks under cover of dark. A rampant singles scene was soon underway, with blacks and whites mingling freely, and everyone eying the opposite sex. Most entertaining were the judges, four staid, middle-aged women who looked like retired headmistresses. Seated behind their imposing table, they were among the few sober members of the crowd. Flowers, ribbons and leaves festooned tables, railings and walls alongside blown-up portraits of the six contestants. Their names alone were worthy of a prize, names such as Ithalia, Latoya, Jasmine and Tallina.

As if to inject a brief note of normality to the proceedings, a small group of first graders dressed in bows, frills and party shoes paraded out with back-up guitar and music director to sing "He's Got the Whole World In His Hands". The remainder of the evening progressed steadily towards debauchery and rowdiness, drowning out the dapper master of ceremonies, dressed impeccably in a white linen suit and hat, who attempted to keep the event moving along with something approaching order. The girls did their thing, appearing first in swim suits that kept you guessing, since each wore a banner wider than the suit was. Progressing through casual wear, evening gown, a dance routine and song, their appearances were greeted with increasingly lewd cheers, particularly for the obvious local favorite. Perhaps in the interests of self-preservation, the judges ultimately crowned the favorite queen, in this case the comely Ithalia.

In the morning, Tristan and Colin were up early and down at The Reach like a shot to survey the damage. We discovered them later, enthusiastically sweeping floors, mopping tables, and filling dust bins along with a slightly hungover morning shift. With the unpredictable taste of teenage boys, they found the aftermath more fun than the event.

*　*　*　*

Hope Town

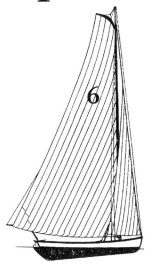

With its narrow paved streets, a maze of pastel clapboarded houses and a profusion of flowers, Hope Town, Elbow Cay typifies the heart of the Abacos. One has a feeling of having stepped back in time, of bringing the glories of the past together with the comforts of the present. The village is lovely and endlessly fascinating, packed tightly along its sheltered harbor, overshadowed by the much photographed candy-stripped lighthouse. A village in miniature, Hope Town possesses a unique charm of its own, a blending of hardworking New England ethic with a Bahamian flair for enjoyment in life.

The Arrival

Getting to Hope Town, our first Abaco destination, involved more than the usual amount of intrigue. First there was the morning water taxi back across the harbor to Eleuthera where we were met by Tom in his infamous pick-up. Then the bone-jarring, bottom-searing trip up to Quartermoon, where we learned our departure had been delayed a day because he had another group he would be flying on to the States. Little alarm bells went off in my head, a sense of disquiet that was reinforced when two particularly large men drove up, apparently to arrange for tomorrow's ride. Obviously, it was going to be one crowded flight.

Arriving at the airport the next morning, we pulled up alongside Tom's plane to be met by not only the two men—who were looking even bigger today—and their copious baggage, but also a massive black Labrador. "Oh God!" moaned Tom, even he momentarily taken aback. "I forgot about the dog." So there we were, five adults, two teenagers, a baby and a dog, all poised to pack inside a delicate aircraft. At least it had two engines; otherwise, we'd probably still be there. Our baggage went in the back, the other guys' gear in the nose. Then everyone squeezed in: the two heavyweights in the back, Tristan, Colin, Gwyneth and me in the center seats, dog on the floor, and Tom and Kevin up front. This had to be the first and last time I'd ever fly with a baby at my breast and a dog drooling on my feet.

Landing at Marsh Harbour, we caught a positively glamorous taxi to the ferry dock, a presentable station wagon with no obvious defects, driven by a sprightly lady in black pants, white shirt and black tie. Bahamians taxi drivers take their role very seriously and are proud of their status as vehicle owners. Vehicles in the Abacos in general, we noticed, were definitely in improved condition. In fact, everything about this northern Out Island group smacked of prosperity, the result of a heritage that sprang from displaced American loyalists rather than a defunct plantation economy. The Abacos possess a charm of their own, one totally unrelated to the remote, self-sufficient, developing life-style of islands like Cat and Long.

We had a final half-hour wait for one of the numerous Albury ferries before crossing to Hope Town where we landed at a small dock in front of a village grocery store. As we would be staying in a villa, buying food was a top priority before the final harbor crossing to Hope Town Hideaway Villas. Little did we know that our quest for food, and bread in particular, would require a call to arms before Easter weekend was over.

*   *   *   *

The Quest for Bread

More than any other holiday, with the possible exception of Ramadan, Easter can throw a monkey wrench into your international travel plans. Arriving in a foreign country, you remember that Easter is just around the corner, but no matter, all that means is religious services, perhaps a parade or two, and children energetically searching for eggs. The casual American tourist does not realize that what seemed like quite a brief holiday at home is capable of extending from Holy Wednesday right through Maundy Thursday, Good Friday, Easter Eve, Easter Sunday, and the final blow— Easter Monday, all cause for stores to close for the duration. The net result is that people indulge in a mad scramble for food and goods, reminiscent of the deluge of humanity that descends on an American supermarket in anticipation of a winter blizzard.

Our first suspicion that Easter might have a greater than normal impact arose on our initial grocery shop. Eager to purchase some of the much advertised whole wheat bread at Vernon's, we tracked down the grocery store with its tiny attendant bakery. While I prowled the small store filled with locals and tourists stocking up for the holidays, Kevin endeavored to locate bread, a truly heroic undertaking as everyone else in Hope Town seemed to be doing the same thing. No, we all were told, the bread wouldn't be ready until afternoon. Every time we returned we heard the same tale, each time smelling the enticing odors of baking, seeing the baker rolling a piece of dough around, but never setting eyes on a baked good. We began to suspect the piece of dough was the same one he'd been rolling around all day. To compound the confusion, one person insisted you couldn't place an order since all bread sales were on a first-come-first-serve basis, whereas others said that the bread presently in the baking process had been claimed.

Back at our villa, as I gazed around the well equipped kitchen in frustration, an inner voice suddenly sounded off in my head, "Bake it yourself, you idiot." Back went Kevin to the store, this time for yeast, flour, and molasses, a procedure that took over an hour and involved two stores, long lines, and near blows. The business of bread was, for the moment, resolved.

* * * *

The Elusive Electricity

Despite its elegant touches, its aura of hominess, its unparalleled setting, Hope Town Hideaways will always remain for us, the place of the elusive electricity. Arriving the previous day, I'd been charmed by the pink villas well integrated into the lush gardens, the winding paths and grassy nooks, the white tiled roofs and wide decks, the spacious interiors and tasteful decor. Most of all I'd loved the kitchen, with its huge stove, generous counters, and immense culinary inventory, including stainless steel pots and pans. Eagerly anticipating some home-cooked meals, we planned menus, stocked up on food, and mixed up a batch of bread. The first morning came off without a hitch, other than the fact that the oven seemed to operate on a permanent low mode. I finally mastered the art of baking by setting it at a whopping 475 degrees.

The first crack in our Utopian armor occurred around mid-afternoon with a power outage, an event shared by not only the entire island , but the neighboring island of Man-O-War as well. As this was apparently a fairly frequent occurrence, it seemed that equipping tourist villas with electric stoves and no back-up generator might be a mistake. On our travels we've experienced numerous power outages, but never have we been without the ability to cook. One lunch and a long walk later, the power was still out, a situation that soon had me seeking an alternative source of tea. Back we went across the harbor in our courtesy whaler to the Harbour's Edge, a restaurant built right in the water with deck seating and boat dockage. Also, I might add, that joy of all joys—a generator. Watching the sun go down, we celebrated the return of electricity as lights twinkled on around the town. Excitement at the prospect of dinner cooking mounted as we motored back across harbor until Kevin, taking stock of the surroundings, pointed out that the Hideaways remained one of the few black spots on the shore. No pretty little lights flanking the garden paths, no welcoming light at the dock, no glowing bulb at each villa entrance. No nothing. Of course, as a final gesture of defiance, the electricity came on just as we were going to bed, long after any of us had any interest in its capabilities.

The next morning we woke in eager anticipation of hot muffins for breakfast, only to find ourselves once again without electricity. By now the scenario was

Hope Town Hideaways, Hope Town

Reservations:	809-366-0224
Direct Phone:	809-366-0224
Direct Fax:	809-366-0451

Location: On the lighthouse side of the harbor (across from the town) in Hope Town, Elbow Cay.

Accommodations: (4) 2-bedroom waterfront villas with fully-equipped kitchens, living-dining area, 2 baths, and large deck.

Getting There: Many airlines service Marsh Harbour airport; take a taxi from the airport to the ferry basin east of Marsh Harbour, then an Albury water taxi to Hope Town.

Local Transport: Albury inter-island ferry service, rental boats, complimentary whaler, and bicycles.

Meals: Self-catering in the villas, or eat in one of several good restaurants in and around Hope Town.

Amenities: Fully equipped villas with decks, a boat dock, a small whaler for in-harbor transport, a rowing dinghy, and a garden area with grill, table and chairs.

Phones: The villas are equipped with phones.

Electricity: Utility electricity from Marsh Harbour (the resort was also reportedly getting a back-up generator for those rare power outages like we experienced!).

Water: The water in the villas is drinkable.

Laundry: Lighthouse marina near the lighthouse.

Food Stores & Restaurants: Good local stores and restaurants in Hope Town, plus the markets and restaurants in Marsh Harbour.

Highlights:

- The beautiful, well-appointed villas. Rarely have we seen a tourist facility so tastefully laid-out and well-integrated into its natural surroundings.

- Plantings are abundant and widely varied.

- The private dock, located just below the villas.

- The waterfront location with great harbor views.

- The privacy yet close proximity to Hope Town.

- The self-sufficiency of having your own fully-equipped villa.

- Peggy Thompson, herself, is one of the Hideaways' main attributes, a fact reflected in the enthusiastic reports offered by previous guests.

strongly reminiscent of our time in the Dominican Republic when electricity went off at night as a matter of course, leaving everyone routinely groping in the dark. Water, on the other hand, came on in the evenings in the Dominican Republic, so even though we couldn't see we could console ourselves with a shower.

We had no hot breakfast, no tea and coffee, no bread baking. In fact, taking inventory of our food stocks, I was alarmed to see there wasn't much we could eat that didn't require some kind of cooking. Next came the inevitable call to Chris, the owner, who at the time was living over in Marsh Harbour. He assured us that help was on the way. Heartened, I optimistically mixed up dough for oatmeal bread, a mistake as it persistently rose, was repeatedly punched down, and finally spent the remainder of the day in the refrigerator where it still continued to rise, showing just how warm even the fridge had become. The fact that most of the rest of the island seemed to be wallowing in electricity didn't help. Peggy, Chris' wife and the person actually in charge of the villas, was currently in the States for minor medical reasons. Her absence left guests feeling more than the usual degree of abandonment. Meeting Peggy later, we could readily believe that her presence would have made a world of difference. Even though this power outage was unusual, Chris was determined to allcviate the situation by installing a back-up generator. Chris and Peggy now live right across the harbor in Hope Town.

Electricity finally returned at six o'clock, thus rescuing a perilous baking and dinner situation. After that, despite its continual comings and goings, we no longer cared. By then I had mastered the art of seizing the moment and cooking furiously, no matter what the hour, even if it meant preparing dinner alongside breakfast.

*   *   *   *

Hope Town Lighthouse

Dominating Hope Town harbor and village is its signature candy-striped lighthouse, an edifice first constructed in the teeth of opposition by local inhabitants. Always a resourceful lot, islanders were at the time profitably employed in the dubious business of wrecking, capitalizing on the many craft that were swept up on the lethal outer barrier reefs. As the presence of a lighthouse would effectively terminate such activities, no one was thrilled at the prospect of having one in the immediate vicinity. They needn't have worried. While the coming of the lighthouse did end wrecking, it ushered in tourism, a business that has been exploiting that charming structure ever since.

Today, Hope Town's lighthouse must be one of the most photographed and visited in the world. In addition to its distinctive candy-striped exterior, it remains one of the few manually operated, kerosene-powered lighthouses still in use, one of two in the Bahamas. A double shift of keepers share the duty of running up and down stairs every few hours around the clock to hand-crank the light mechanism, a formidable task given the one hundred steps up the steep, narrow stairwell. Visitors are welcome to explore the premises, climbing to a magnificent view across the Abaco Triangle of islands. For the intrepid, there's even an outer balcony, reached via a small, low crawlspace, built to the proportions of a midget. No visitor should miss this opportunity to see both the lighthouse in use and its aerial view.

* * * *

Bessie's Bakery & The Birthday

Years ago, when we first visited Hope Town on our sailboat, Bessie's Bakery reigned supreme, enjoying accolades that traveled from boat to boat. Eulogies honored the fabled bread, the cinnamon buns, the pies. We never made it there, as our boat was already well equipped for baking, something I have enjoyed doing. Subsequent years saw a shift in bakery demographics, from Bessie's (an aging enterprise) to Vernon's, progressively located in the center of town rather than down a small harbor channel, reached only by boat. Bessie's seemed a forgotten enterprise, forgotten, that is, until my birthday.

Having been born in April, I find that my birthday invariably arrives while we're on a trip, a situation that means I never have it in the same country twice. Never, that is, until the Bahamas. Not only would this year experience the first repeat birthday nation, but it was the very town where I had enjoyed a birthday ten years earlier. Back then, Tristan and Colin had been docile little tots with hardly an ambition in the world. Now at the progressive age of fourteen, they wanted full control of my birthday preparations.

Waking on my birthday with a sense of mission, they soon had Kevin in tow, herding him about town in a frenzy of activity. Presents were bought, treats prepared, decorations made, and a cake sought. A cake, it soon evolved, was asking too much on this of all weekends. Being Easter, there wasn't a cake to be found anywhere, particularly at the overworked Vernon's Bakery. How about special cookies, Kevin suggested, or ice cream, or some other treat. Obstinate to the core, the children pursued a cake, something, as they put it, you could have candles in. By four p.m. panic had set in, with still no cake in sight. "What about Bessie's?," Tristan said. Putting out feelers, they learned that the baker there was old, his productivity fitful, the results varied. "Who cares," the boys declared. "Let's go." The dinghy was fetched and off they all went, all of this totally unknown to me.

Arriving at the private dock located up a creek, they proceeded up to the house to be greeted by an ancient man, a man who looked as though baking had been beyond his capabilities for years. "Do you have any cake?" the boys asked hopefully.

"No," he quavered, his voice barely audible. "Just some bread." A gnarled hand reached across the table to reveal a handful of white loaves resting under a dish cloth.

"What about something sweet," they continued, still on a wave of optimism. "It's for a birthday."

"I bake pies in the morning," he replied, after a thoughtful pause. The boys were crestfallen, explaining that the birthday was that evening. Without a moment's hesitation he began reaching for pie plate and oleo stick, leaping into action like a man half his age.

"Come back in an hour," he shot at them as they retreated from the onslaught of culinary activity. Thus was born my birthday Key Lime pie, a delicious concoction begun at five o'clock, finished by six, and devoured by bedtime, a fitting end to another perfect overseas birthday.

*   *   *   *

Island Entertainment

Hope Town offers a wide variety of entertainment in this minute, exquisitely beautiful village. A lonely stretch of white sand beach lines the Atlantic side, while a compact cluster of narrow streets (too narrow for cars), tiny shops, lovely cottages and profusion of flowers border the protected harbor. Many of the houses and streets have colorful names: Butterfly House, Spinney

The Hope Town Harbour Lodge, Hope Town

Reservations:	800-316-7844 (US)
Direct Phone:	809-366-0095
Direct Fax:	809-366-0286

Location: On the ocean/town side of the harbor in Hope Town, Elbow Cay.

Accommodations: The lodge has 20 double rooms with views of the ocean, pool, or harbor, and the Butterfly house rental has accommodations for 4 persons.

Getting There: Fly to Marsh Harbour International Airport, taxi to Albury's ferry located east of town for the twice-daily water taxi service to the Harbour Lodge.

Local Transport: Albury inter-island ferry service, rental boats, and bicycles.

Meals: MAP or by the meal; breakfast on the patio, lunch served poolside, and dinner in the dining room (closed Thursday evenings for local darts competition!).

Amenities: Large pool, bar and restaurant, ferry dock and immediate ocean access.

Phones: There is a direct line at the hotel office and pay phones in town.

Electricity: Utility electricity from Marsh Harbour.

Water: The water in the hotel is drinkable.

Laundry: The hotel has a laundry service and there is a laundromat at the Lighthouse Marina across the harbor.

Food Stores & Restaurants: Good local stores and restaurants in Hope Town, plus markets and restaurants in Marsh Harbour.

Highlights:

- The central location in the heart of Hope Town, within easy walking distance of shops and restaurants.

- The immediate access to the ocean beach.

- The great harbor and ocean views from the hotel grounds.

- The large pool with bar and restaurant service just a few steps away from the beach.

- The Old-World charm of the hotel and the friendliness of the staff.

- The rooms are small, but recently renovated with bright, cheery decor and comfortable furnishings.

Dune, Puff House, Toad Hall. Walking, you find yourself passing down Lover's Lane, Well Lane, or Malone Street, named for one of the founding families. The sense of history is well defined, from the recurrent family names to the New England architecture and the Old World lilt of the islander's talk. As with Harbour Island, the cottages feature gingerbread eaves, shuttered windows, pastel trim and picket fences. Cisterns, fed by an elaborate system of gutters and pipes, are the island's sole water source, the older ones situated in back yards while newer homes have them incorporated into the foundation.

More can be learned about island history from the Wyannie Malone Historic Museum, filled with local memorabilia from the history of Hope Town (wrecking, rope-making, sponging, boatbuilding, lumbering, tourism) to local handicrafts. Outside stand various artifacts: a pump, a rain catching device and cistern, a wooden boat, an outhouse, a beehive oven, and a rope making display. The boys remarked on the similarities of the things we see repeatedly in our travels. The pump was like the one we used in Nova Scotia, the rope-making like that we saw in Guatemala, the oven like the one in a Costa Rican bakery, the outhouse like any number of others around the world. You really couldn't ask for a better education than the one they were getting through travel, one that not only taught them about life, but showed the interconnection between cultures all over the world.

Later, the contrast between our children's enthusiasm at the museum and some people's reaction to a place like the Bahamas was exemplified by a conversation we overheard outside the town medical clinic, the site of one of the few public phones. Standing with her husband, and speaking in strident tones into the phone was an attractive woman in her thirties. Her tanned face radiated discontent as she conversed with what must have been a friend back in the States.

"You wouldn't believe how primitive and isolated it is out here," she complained loudly, immediately catching our attention from our spot on the clinic porch. Never in our wildest dreams would we have described Hope Town as either primitive or isolated. In fact, despite its compact size and historic flavor, the place was as modern as many stateside villages. Listening with growing interest, we heard her continue the lament. "There's no TV, no phone, nothing for the kids to do except swim at the beach." She made it sound like the depths of deprivation. "We have a motorboat, but there's nowhere to go, it's so isolated." Taking into account the abundant houses, the numerous shops and restaurants, the packed anchorage and plentiful walks, it was hard to feel sympathetic. Now if this had been Cat Island, she might have had a valid complaint. "The kids are bored out of their minds with no television," she moaned. Clearly, her definition of primitive meant no TV, while isolated probably was defined as no phone. "And you know that girl we brought with us—that little friend? Well, she had a cold, so now we're all sick." She paused to let this final death knell to the holiday sink in. "I don't know what the kids are all going to do. They'd call some friends, only we don't have a phone." The cry was from the heart, an inability to cope with life without a television, telephone, or car.

Having wrung all the sympathy she could from her friend, she next called a local car rental place in her desperate quest to go somewhere. I could have told her there was nowhere to go. If she thought Hope Town was a wasteland, the other end of the island was going to be a real shock. Hanging up after a brief inquiry with the car rental company, she turned to her husband. "I guess we'll just have to go out in the boat again," was her parting remark. One could just sense that this wasn't going to be a hit with the kids.

* * * *

Medical Clinic

Each Out Island has a medical clinic in its main town, a small, unobtrusive building that periodically enjoys a visit from a traveling physician. We'd seen them everywhere, usually closed, with the doctor's visiting days posted on the door, never needing them until Tristan developed a persistent swimmer's ear. Seeking out the one in Hope Town, we checked the schedule and learned that the doctor came every Monday at nine o'clock. Arriving on time, we found two people already seated on the front porch waiting for the doctor to arrive. One, a spry, gray-haired lady of obvious New England vintage, was there in the guise of volunteer, while the other, an elderly local woman by the name of Mrs. Cash was busy filling in the time by relating a catalogue of her ills. By nine-thirty, with still no doctor in sight, she began to look agitated. "I told them I'd be late for work, but I didn't say I wouldn't be coming to work at all," she said with a touch of asperity. "The thing is, I really need more of my pills. There's only one left." She shook the empty bottle as if for effect.

"What seems to be the problem," her companion asked, having obviously lost track during the previous catalogue of ailments.

"It's my blood," Mrs Cash stated. "I had this shock, you see. Lost the feeling in my right arm for a while."

"Really?", the other woman said companionably.

"Yes, this arm right here." A plump limb was raised

for perusal. "It was salt," she added. "Too much of it in my diet. They said I would have ulcers if I kept on."

By now she had my attention. It isn't every day you hear diabetes, a stroke and heart trouble mentioned all in one diagnosis. That must have been quite a pill she was waiting for. Mrs. Cash soon departed in a flurry for work, her companion off home to call Man-O-War and find out what happened to the doctor. Returning five minutes later she gave Tristan and me the bad news. The doctor, a winter resident from Maine, had gone sailing instead of keeping her appointed rounds. Just then an old woman, rail thin and possessed of that weathered look one associates with the Depression years, appeared at the clinic steps. Every line of her thin, hard body bristled with indignation at finding the doctor absent.

"I need my medicine," she said with an air of finality.

"Well I'm sorry, Lilly, but I'm not a doctor," the other woman explained patiently. Lilly looked at her in disbelief, as though the doctor's absence was a personal conspiracy.

"I'll die without my medicine," she exclaimed, almost as though she expected to drop dead on the spot.

Then with a final parting glare, she turned and stalked away. By the look of things, Lilly still had plenty of life left in her.

* * * *

Man-O-War

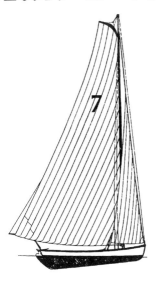

More than any other Out Island, Man-O-War has
experienced change. Once the wooden boat-building
capital of the Bahamas, it has now turned mostly to
building fiberglass power boats and new homes, to
providing marine services of all types, and to developing
locally produced crafts. The prosperous exclusively
white population, descendents of original settlers, is
characterized by a strong religious tradition that mani-
fests itself in a modesty of clothing, a self-containment, a
simple, hard-working life-style. The island itself is
lovely, easily explored on foot, and enjoyable for those
who seek a quiet retreat.

The Arrival

Late one afternoon we took the ferry from Hope
Town to Man-O-War, riding on one of the many
"Donnies". All ferries in the Abaco Triangle between

Marsh Harbour, Man-O-War and Hope Town are named "Donnie", with assorted identifying Roman numerals after them. Skippered by a variety of local men, from the dour to the solicitous, they ply the waters with all the dependability of an energetic team of workhorses. While we shared ours with only two other passengers, these ferries provide a much used source of transportation for visiting tourists, school children and commuting workers. A ride on one is worth the money just for the wonderful water view it gives of the passing islands. And no island approach is more exciting than Man-O-War, barreling in the narrow cut that appears as if by magic in mid-island, opening into two all-weather harbors.

We were met at the ferry dock by Brenda Sawyer, the young, pleasant owner-manager of Schooners Landing, the only formal tourist accommodations on Man-O-War. Whisked off in a tiny mini-van, we quickly noticed that vehicles on the island, although in short supply, were of an entirely different quality than those in the rest of the Out Islands. Here, the unusually narrow streets required a certain ingenuity of vehicle, while island prosperity resulted in their impeccable condition. As we remembered from previous visits, the waterfront area still teemed with activity, mainly the marinas and boatyards for which Man-O-War has a long-standing tradition. Pointing out one of the two grocery stores in town at the end of the road, Brenda headed uphill, climbing to the incongruously named "Queens Highway", a road built to the proportions of a sidewalk. From there we headed north out of town, taking the dirt track that doubles as a road, servicing the many private homes tucked along either shore.

Arriving at the small hotel complex just outside of town, we gazed in amazement. Somehow, in arranging two months of accommodations, we must have become confused. Expecting to find a small resort ("Do you think we'll have two rooms?" the boys had asked hopefully) we found ourselves presented with an entire condominium-style villa. Two rooms? We had two floors! Thank goodness I'd brought along all that food I'd never managed to cook in Hope Town due to the frequent power shortages. Throwing together the makings of a curry, I relaxed in the spacious surroundings, thrilled to be back on the island we remembered so fondly from our sailing days.

* * * *

Food & Shopping

Food shopping on Man-O-War is among the best in the Out Islands, the result of a prosperous, organized community and good location. Because of their proximity, goods are shipped directly to the Abacos from Florida, thus avoiding the disorganization and price hike that typifies the Nassau connection. Even the ubiquitous Donnies which carry local supplies are an island enterprise, owned and operated by the Albury family. While Marsh Harbour still serves as the main supply center, shopping on Man-O-War is fun and easy, with the efficiency and variety of larger communities.

Provisioning for five days, we discovered it was necessary to visit both grocery stores, a piece of advice Brenda had offered on our arrival. She was right. It was almost as though the two stores had collaborated and decided not to carry the same things. Albury's, located on the Queens Highway, delivers to your door or boat, a convenience for those who don't want to backpack everything home afterwards.

Schooner's Landing, Man-O-War

Reservations:	809-365-6072
Direct Phone:	809-365-6072
Direct Fax:	809-365-6285

Location: Schooner's Landing is located on the north shore of Man-O-War Cay, a short distance from the town center.

Accommodations: There are four condominium-style rental units in one waterfront building. Each unit has two bedrooms and one-and-a-half baths, a fully-equipped kitchen, living-dining area, and a large terrace. There is a three-night minimum stay.

Getting There: Many airlines service Marsh Harbour airport; take a taxi from the airport to the Albury ferry basin east of Marsh Harbour, then a water taxi to Man-O-War Cay. Guests are picked up at the dock and taken to the resort by mini-van.

Local Transport: Walking and resort shuttle van.

Meals: Self-catering in the rental units, or Brenda Sawyer can arrange to have meals prepared.

Amenities: The amenities include a fully-equipped villa, immediate access to the beach, dock privileges, and local transport.

Phones: There are pay phones located in town.

Electricity: Man-O-War Cay gets its utility electricity from Marsh Harbour.

Water: The water at the resort is drinkable.

Laundry: The resort has a laundry facility and there is a laundromat at the marina in town.

Food Stores & Restaurants: There are several good local food stores and a few local restaurants, plus the markets and restaurants in Marsh Harbour and Hope Town.

Highlights:

• The villa units are well-appointed and comfortable.

• The waterfront location is spectacular, and the uniqueness of Man-O-War Cay makes a visit interesting.

• The privacy and quiet surroundings, yet close proximity to town.

• The hospitality of co-owner/manager Brenda Sawyer; she can arrange transport, groceries, catered dinners and laundry.

• Children can be very comfortable and relaxed here, although a strong north or east wind in winter can make the ocean beach untenable.

For baked goods, we discovered two home-based operations, the inevitable Alburys and Sawyers (Brenda's mother-in-law) whose specialties included cinnamon buns. Brenda also sold fresh-baked bread at her attractive souvenir shop next to Albury's Grocery. As we found nothing in the way of whole wheat bread, I was soon once again baking rigorously to keep up with the boys' voracious appetites, this time using a casserole dish and an oven that was too hot. The variety in the shape of the loaves and the consistency of texture was always a source of amusement.

For those who don't want to bother with preparing dinner, Brenda can arrange for home-cooked meals, an island specialty, to be delivered to Schooner's Landing at reasonable prices.

Man-O-War is a dry island, because of religious conviction. The thought of no alcohol, no drink in hand as the sun sets, no glass of wine with dinner, is enough to send many holiday seekers scurrying in the opposite direction. It's true that there are no atmospheric waterfront restaurants with quaint pubs like those you find in Hope Town, but for those who like to escape the tourist scene and enjoy the peace of island living, it's no problem. You can always bring your own alcoholic beverages, or Brenda can arrange to have whatever you want shipped over from Hope Town on the ferry. If you choose to drink, have respect for local custom and be discrete.

* * * *

Island Impressions

Kevin and I (with baby) were walking the island one Sunday morning when we encountered a golf cart traffic jam on the Queens Highway as islanders headed to church—men in trousers and colorful shirtsleeves, women in dresses, often with a lace handkerchief pinned to their hair, girls in frills and bows. Further down the road stood the Church of God. Its roadside was lined with parked golf carts, the favored mode of transportation around town, even when going only a block or two. To the casual visitor, many of the island residents seem to look alike; in fact many of them are cousins. While at first impression the islanders seem to keep to themselves, evincing little interest in visitors, their hospitality is extended to those who stay a while.

Unlike Hope Town, where much of the historic flavor of the village has been retained, Man-O-War has experienced a general modernization of homes, a replacement of small, compact gardens with wide unproductive expanses of lawn. No one seems to walk or bicycle, preferring the comfort of golf carts, and children are noticeably absent from the streets. Prosperity has obviously taken its toll, resulting in a younger generation that tends to be overweight and is often lacking in the strong work ethic that formed the cornerstone of the island. Few, if any, young people have interest in continuing the wooden boat building trade for which the island has such a reputation. The focus has shifted to fiberglass boat building, marine services and house construction. Still, as Brenda pointed out, they will soon have to look for other forms of employment as available land is practically used up. So far, tourism has been limited to providing small shops, frequented by day trippers arriving from Hope Town and Marsh Harbour.

Our general impression, given a ten year absence, was that Man-O-War isn't as quaint as it used to be. Footpaths at the end of the island have been widened to accommodate vehicles, the waterfront area has lost some of its appeal, and even the remaining handful of old homes have received a modernizing face-lift. Colorful gardens, picket fences and dense tropical vegetation have often given way to green lawns and a sprinkling of artfully placed shrubs, a suburban veneer that seems out of place in the Out Islands. If Man-O-War's economy ever does depend more on tourism, it may live to regret this trend that is in contrast to the village's original character.

* * * *

Island Walks

Continuing beyond the Queens Highway, we picked up the well-remembered footpath that runs from the village down the southern portion of the island to South Harbour. Practically around the first corner loomed a new home that made other modern touches pale in comparison, a grotesque monstrosity aptly named Outrageous. With its name boldly outlined in gold-edged letters adorning a flowing scroll above the door, the impression was of unparalleled ostentation: tall white pillars, a gaudy coat-of-arms plastered to an outside wall, white, crushed stone drive, and a lawn that looked as though it was flown in from Florida.

Once past this masterpiece we enjoyed lovely scenery and excellent hiking along the groomed track almost to the tip of the island. Footpaths led off to waterfront homes, glimpses of blue water penetrated the dense undergrowth, and suddenly we were looking out at our favorite Abaco anchorage where we had spent so many weeks during our earlier travels by sailboat.

Better yet was the walk to the north end of the island, continuing along the track that leads beyond Schooners Landing. A sandy path with little traffic, lined with tall pines and coconut palms, it possesses a mysterious, untamed appearance. Here the homes are well integrated and nature allowed to run riot with a refreshing freedom. One stretch, lined on both sides with a hedge of evergreens, made us feel as though we were walking through an emerald corridor. Numerous bells stood mounted beside footpath entrances to homes, their elegance reminiscent of some Mediterranean villa. At one spot the island narrowed to a rocky spit, leaving the lush vegetation of the island center for a final section of sand and windswept shrubs. Walking the route out and back took an hour and a half from Schooners Landing, a perfect distance in the heat and with children. Afterwards, we ended with a cool-off swim at a harborside dock, as strong onshore winds made the oceanside beach untenable.

* * * *

Island Shopping

Man-O-War is known throughout the Abacos for its shops. Scattered about the town (most of the waterfront area is given over to the boatbuilding and marine service trade) are a handful of island shops, carrying inexpensive souvenirs and expensive, well crafted island-made products. In one tiny hole-in-the-wall, a woman fashioned batik outfits; at another a variety of family members sewed colorful bags, hats, purses and duffels from heavy-duty canvas; another displayed hand-carved wooden models, hand-knit sweaters, home-baked goods and hand-crafted jewelry. With a total of about five shops, the variety was extensive, the quality top notch, perfectly suited to those with a flexible budget and a yen for browsing.

Most popular with the boys was the waterfront take-out restaurant where we indulged in delicious ice cream cones. Sitting outside at the adjoining table, I probably left a lasting impression on the conservative island by nursing Gwyneth Islay, a practice islanders consider archaic, if not downright embarrassing. Perhaps nothing exemplified more the difference in attitude between black and white Bahamian islands than this. On the southern islands, I had been the envy of mothers because I breast-fed my baby (many of them worked away from the house), while here, among a group of industrious, "progressive" whites, my nursing was considered backward. Breast-feeding, like other common-sense customs discarded in the name of progress, has made a comeback in the past few years, and possibly will in this part of the Bahamas. It seems that mankind develops in a circle, continuing along a path that eventually brings him back to where he began, a comforting thought in this era of frequent change.

* * * *

Marsh Harbour

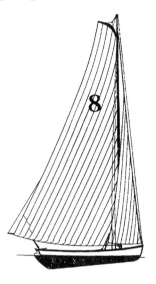

The hub of the Abacos, Marsh Harbour serves as the supply center for the northern Out Islands. Airports and ferries, shops and services originate here in this small yet bustling town. For those who like action, the hotels and resorts, restaurants and bars supply plenty of nightlife. While the town lacks the charm and historic appeal of its neighbors, Marsh Harbour offers a less expensive base for day outings to the surrounding islands, either by ferry or rental boat. Above all, Marsh Harbour is a boating center, with charter outfits, marinas, well stocked stores, and a large, all-weather harbor.

The Arrival

We made the crossing to Marsh Harbour, then caught another taxi ride, this time with a lively woman sporting a straw hat perched jauntily on top of abundant dyed-red hair. At first glance, Pelican Beach Villas seemed a bit odd, with only the day maids on the premises. Ada, a large, friendly black woman seemed to be in charge, checking each day to see if everything was okay as she delivered fresh towels and executed a quick cleaning. The villas themselves were old but comfortable and well equipped, their only real drawback being a fascinating assortment of ill-fitting screens. The setting was delightfully quiet, situated among a group of casuarinas beside a small beach, with a view out towards Man-O-War Cay. Coming from the dramatic setting of Schooners Landing, we no longer felt two steps from falling in the ocean, far better for babies and children that like to putter on the beach.

*   *   *   *

Provisioning

As mentioned before, Marsh Harbour is an excellent place to provision, with two excellent grocery stores that carry just about everything you could want. All stores and services are well stocked because they get direct delivery from Florida without having to deal with the inefficiency of Nassau. Prices are lower as well. Our favorite store was the Family Market, a small operation on main street that sells Abaco-grown produce at bargain prices and an assortment of home-baked goods. The irony is that here you can buy all sorts of inexpensive, locally-grown produce, while right over on the other cays, produce is pricey and almost exclusively imported from the States. Why buy a Florida orange if you can get an Abaco one? For that matter, why buy an apple that came all the way from the state of Washington? The owners of the Family Market found that the key to supply was organizing pick-up from the farms themselves, thus encouraging local growers to keep productive.

As a boating center, Marsh Harbour has all the usual marine services, including a complete line of boat equipment, albeit on a smaller scale than what you might find in a place like Florida. In fact, it's the small scale that makes dealing with Marsh Harbour so appealing, with city services supplied in a country setting. Medical services, including a fully-staffed clinic, are also available right in town.

*   *   *   *

Transportation

No matter how you look at it, walking in Marsh Harbour is pretty unpleasant. With no sidewalks in many places, too many cars, and a lack of scenic surroundings, walking seems more a chore than a pleasure. Continuing out beyond our villa along the upscale Pelican Shores housing development proved quiet, although the scenery was a far cry from the usual quaint homes and undisturbed landscapes of other Out Island explorations. Walking a sleeping baby, I discovered that huge homes were the norm, habitually attended by vast lawns, vigorous guard dogs, prominently displayed No Trespassing-Private Property signs, and the inevitable Haitian garden crew.

While walking or bicycling the Marsh Harbour area is of minimal interest compared to the outlying islands, renting a small motorboat, riding the public ferries, or chartering a sailboat are all great ways to enjoy the best of the Abacos. One truly adventurous undertaking would be a bicycle trip from Marsh Harbour down the length of Great Abaco to Sandy Point on its southern tip, thus experiencing some of the most remote areas in the Out Islands.

* * * *

Travels With Children: Treasure Cay Exploits

While staying in Marsh Harbour we finally met Peggy Thompson, owner and manager of Hope Town Hideaways. An American girl who married into one of the oldest families in the Abacos, Peggy was for us one of the more entertaining people it's been our pleasure to meet. Small, pretty and vivacious, she seemed born to talk. As she put it, "If there's someone to talk to, I'll keep talking." One of those easy-going people with a knack for enjoying life, nothing seemed to faze her. It was easy to see how her presence at the Hideaways would make a world of difference. Full of energy and ideas, Peggy descended on us our second day in Marsh Harbour, arriving in an aged, battered sedan with four-year-old Jade and eight-week-old Shannon in tow, bearing gifts of garden vegetables and toys for Gwyneth to play with. She then suggested an outing to Treasure Cay Beach, the best beach on Great Abaco.

The day of the outing dawned, with Kevin bowing out at the final moment, a good move as it turned out to be strictly a women and children kind of affair. We took off at noon in her mother-in-law's car, a capacious American stationwagon, complete with roof rack and backseat that Peggy couldn't quite figure out. The four of us squeezed into the middle seat, leaving the front for Peggy, Jade and Shannon. Off we went in a cloud of dust, with a first stop at the aforementioned mother-in-law's. Borrowing the car, it seemed wasn't enough.

"We need a spare tire in case of a flat—the island roads are lethal," Peggy explained. "Of course," she added, "we don't have a jack. But you can always flag down a car and borrow a jack, I figure. Having the tire seems the more important item, don't you think?" Having both would have been totally unBahamian.

The required spare was located from a pile of assorted household items stored in the car park, then wrestled to the roof by Tristan and Colin. Next, Peggy ventured into the equally cluttered backyard to wrest a cafe umbrella from its parent picnic table, thinking that Shannon needed some shade at the beach. This, too, was hoisted to the rooftop and tied down by assorted bits of rope. One could only hope the mysterious mother-in-law didn't open the umbrella over some ladies' luncheon in the future and unsuspectingly dump a bucket full of sand on the proceedings. Last of all, Peggy dashed inside for lunch. A lunch, not made by her, but by her mother-in-law, of course. The mother-in-law took care of all—picnic lunches, assorted vehicles, spare tires and beach umbrellas. Evening dinners as well, I was willing to bet.

The second stop was the airport to drop off lunch with her husband, Chris, then on to pick up Jade at her private "school". Not a playgroup, mind you.

"All that Jade learned at playgroup was how to want things," Peggy explained. "Like the shoes she came home wanting, those kind with lights on them. Okay, I thought, how bad can the price of shoes for a four-year-old be. So I went to the store and, you know, they were forty dollars. Well, I figured when the lights burned out I could replace the batteries and save them for Shannon. But the salesman said "Forget it. You can't replace the batteries." When they give out, people just throw them away. Forty dollars for a four-year-old just to throw

Pelican Beach Villas, Marsh Harbour

Reservations:	800-642-7268
Direct Phone:	809-367-3600
Fax (US):	912-437-6223

Location: Across the harbour from the town on the waterfront in Pelican Shores.

Accommodations: 2-bedroom waterfront villas with fully-equipped kitchens, living-dining area, baths, and deck.

Getting There: Many airlines service Marsh Harbour airport; take a taxi from the airport to Pelican Shores.

Local Transport: Albury inter-island ferry service, taxis, rental cars and boats, and bicycles.

Meals: Self-catering in the villas, or eat in one of many good restaurants in and around Marsh Harbour.

Amenities: fully-equipped villas, immediate access to shallow beach, protected dock.

Phones: The villas are equipped with phones and share a single phone line.

Electricity: Utility electricity.

Water: The water in the villas is drinkable.

Laundry: There is a laundry on the premises and laundromats in town.

Food Stores & Restaurants: There are good local food stores, supermarkets and restaurants.

Highlights:

- Pelican Beach Villas manages to enjoy a quiet spot in a normally busy corner of the Abacos.

- The privacy, yet close proximity to stores and restaurants in town.

- The great view out across the water toward Man-O-War Cay.

- The immediate access to a shallow beach area and the Mermaid man-made snorkeling reef a short distance away.

- The well-protected boat dock.

them away? You've got to be kidding! That's good marketing for you."

In fact, modern trends are wrapped up neatly for me in Peggy's story of the "electric shoes". The power of marketing on our social value system is terrifying. Not that parents need succumb, but most prefer the easier route of providing whatever it is their children think they want.

Looking like refugees with car and roof rack filled to capacity, we continued on to Treasure Cay Beach, following the arrow-straight road that runs the length of Great Abaco between Cooper's Town in the north and Marsh Harbour. Well paved and almost perfectly flat, the road was flanked by a seemingly endless expanse of tall, slender Madeira pines, once the backbone of a thriving lumber industry. During its heyday, a railroad was operated on the island, transporting the cut lumber to the coast for shipment.

Treasure Cay isn't really a "cay", but a thin peninsula that curves away from the bulk of Great Abaco. Edged by one of the most spectacular Bahamian beaches, it was developed into an enormous resort complex, complete with hotel, restaurant, marina, golf course and villas. Even a village of sorts sprung up in the area, comprising wintering Northerners and hired help. Having once stopped off on our boat for a brief visit, we had found the establishment unappealing and sterile as huge resorts tend to be, with no sense of cultural identity. Now the resort stood closed, its demise a reflection of people's changing tastes as they sought a more intimate contact with the places they traveled to. Apparently the marina was still operational and a number of villas were now in private hands, but the whole place projected a sense of being misplaced, out of keeping with the rest of the Abacos. The beach, however, remained with its beauty largely unchanged as Treasure Cay homeowners, with their assorted jet skis and windsurfers, seemed to confine themselves to a single corner at one end.

If our departure from Marsh Harbour was entertaining, our arrival at the beach more than equalled it. By now Tristan and Colin were strongly suspecting they'd been brought along purely for their brawn, as they lugged beach umbrella and towels, blanket and baby's bassinet, plus an enormous crate of toys. They could only be thankful that the large cooler, packed with enough food and drink to supply a marathon race, was left behind in the car.

Peggy spent her first half hour accompanying Jade into the sand dunes, leaving me in charge of an increasingly bored Shannon in her bassinet. Cooing and smiling energetically in my efforts to entertain her, I suddenly glanced from this sweet, docile, helpless two-month-old towards my daughter who was standing possessively over the toy crate, stark naked except for her sunhat, screeching with delight as she heaved toy after toy out into the sand. The contrast between the two, separated by a mere six months, seemed unbelievable, a startling transition from helpless infant to barely-controlled toddler.

Peggy no sooner returned from the sand dune episode than she found herself dealing with a restless baby. "Why isn't she sleeping?" she complained. Jade, alert to her mother's reoccupation with infant sister, set off down the beach in obvious defiance. Orders to return only sped up the process until she disappeared into the dunes. Meanwhile, my offspring were conducting themselves with admirable restraint, the boys playing happily and Gwyneth chortling from her position amidst the crate of toys.

"How come yours are so good and mine so awful?" Peggy remarked.

Perhaps it was all the travel they did, with its exposure to strangers and different cultures, but the children had all acquired early the ability to behave themselves in public.

"Don't worry," I assured Peggy. "They have their moments."

The return trip some hours later began with a loading of everyone, all the beach gear, and mounds of sand into the car. Peggy embarked on a side trip to show us a blue hole she had once visited, located rather vaguely somewhere off in the forest near the Treasure Cay airport. Plunging down a dirt track, we drove through miles of woods, all to no avail, finally executed a heroic U-turn in a car that was wider than the road, and headed off down yet another, even narrower path deeper into the forest. Passing a couple of abandoned cars, I could only hope we didn't get a flat. Flagging down a passing car to borrow a jack didn't seem like a likely prospect. Getting lost, however, was never a threat.

By the time we abandoned the blue hole quest and headed back into town, both Gwyneth Islay and Jade were fast asleep, a blissful state that lasted until Shannon's growing hunger drove her into a high decibel level of crying. Peggy had completely forgotten that she'd planned to nurse the baby at the blue hole.

"Do you want me to nurse her?" I suggested. Peggy looked startled, then rather smitten with the idea.

"Why not," she agreed.

Why not, indeed. She was stuck driving, the baby was howling its head off, and here I was loaded with milk. Passing a satiated Gwyneth over to Colin on the far side of the back seat, I soon had a contented Shannon drinking away daintily. One look at that interloper at my breast and Gwyneth went off into the tantrum of all tantrums, howling, throwing herself around, and making a determined effort to crawl across the boys to me. Her passionate jealousy abated only when I finally traded babies and offered her not only a breast, but *the* breast, the one Shannon had drunk from. Gwyneth was staking her claim. From then on it was musical babies as I switched back and forth, pacifying each in turn.

To say that Peggy took the return trip at a clip is an understatement. Once back in Marsh Harbor again, she dropped us off with an airy farewell. Regarding the sand-filled car, the quantities of beach paraphernalia, the fussy baby and tired toddler, she gave us a cheery grin as though she hadn't a care in the world. While dinner preparations still loomed ahead for us, she already had her catering service lined up. Climbing back into the car, she shot us a parting remark, letting us in on her secret to success, her formula for the ultimate in relaxed living.

"I think," she remarked decisively, " I'll go over to my mother-in-law's house and get some help."

*   *   *   *

Abaco Stories

Among her many attributes, Peggy proved to be a wealth of information regarding the history of the area. From her we learned that Marsh Harbour was originally just a strip of shops where the freighter delivered goods from which the outer cays provisioned. From these humble beginnings it grew rapidly, fueled by the surplus population from the smaller cays as limited space forced them to relocate, bringing their enterprises with them. Finally, the government center moved there from Hope Town, thus establishing Marsh Harbour as the pivotal

point in the Abacos. Hope Town itself once had a population of about 2,500 (its current year round population is
just under 300). In those days, homes were built so close
together that a woman could knock on her wall and
summon the neighbor next door. Great Abaco provided
much needed space for garden plots as well as fresh
water wells if rains were scarce and cisterns ran dry in
Hope Town. Eventually, in the twenties a huge group of
inhabitants relocated to Key West in Florida following
two back-to-back hurricanes that devastated the Abacos.
Peggy said the reason everyone on Man-O-War, Hope
Town and Marsh Harbour looks so much alike is because
many are cousins, descended from the handful of original families that settled the area. Names such as Albury,
Lowe, Russel, Sawyer, Thompson, Sweeting and Malone
appear over and over again throughout the Abaco
Triangle.

Another one of her stories, in which she describes the
lyrics of a popular song, illustrates the more laidback
approach to marriage of the black Bahamian culture, at
variance with the rigid moral fiber of some of the white
Abaco Bahamians. The story tells of two young Bahamians who fall in love. Learning of this, the father tells his
son confidentially, "You can't marry her because, although your mother doesn't know it, she's your sister."
The young man is so depressed that his mother, sensitive
to her son's distress, finally gets the story out of him.
"That's no problem," she says, "because, although your
father doesn't know it, you're not his son."

* * * *

Cooking with Electricity—Bahamas Style

Electric stoves seem to be the norm in rental villas, a
situation that led to many an unexpected development

for one who, like myself, is accustomed to dealing with gas. Beginning with the Hidaways fiasco, I progressed through a number of bread-baking scenarios before peaking at Pelican Beach villas. There, my bread finally assumed a familiar shape and texture, suggesting that I was finally getting a handle on this electric oven business. Not on the burners, though. So far I'd managed to over and under cook things, as well as fry our complete camp pot set, all by turning the wrong burners off or on. It's amazing how confusing those five little knobs can get when you're used to the instant response of a gas burner. You think you've turned a burner off only to discover it has stuck on "high", or you've turned a burner on and find out it was the one the nest of stored pots was sitting on, all of which were quietly frying their plastic handles into a gooey mess while your tea water remained stone cold. The ovens at Pelican Beach, however, worked like a charm, once you'd made sure it was really the oven that was turned on. Most challenging was trying to use more than one burner at once. You want the rice to steam and the eggs to boil, only you find you've turned the eggs on low and the rice on high. You return from a companionable, pre-dinner drink on the patio to find the eggs have ceased to cook all together, while the rice is glued in a blackened mass to the bottom of the pan. Kevin was incredulous over my ineptness until he did the same thing. For anyone accustomed to the finer points of electric stove cookery, I suppose all this is child's play. But if not, and you intend to rent a villa, be forewarned. Cooking with electricity could provide you with some of your most unexpected adventures.

* * * *

The Changing of the Guard

We were just laying out lunch one day when Ada came and apologetically told us the owner—currently living in Georgia—wanted us to relocate to villa #2 so some newly arriving guests could use #1. Villa #2, it seemed, had a defunct refrigerator and a temporary small one in its place, a defect the owner seemed more inclined to inflict on visiting writers than on normal guests. Perhaps these were special friends of the owner, or even relatives. Whatever the reason, we moved, sweeping our way out of one villa and into the next, all the while speculating on the new arrivals. We took an inventory of both villas as we decided to pool our resources in the name of inconvenience (especially as the whole crib had to be dismantled to get it out the bedroom door). The cookie sheet, cutting board, doormat and dishrack went with us. Also the ice. Jockeying all our food into the minute refrigerator took some doing, especially as this one had no freezer. With the move finally completed, we all admitted we liked the new villa better: more sunlight, a better view front and back, quieter, and a better dish and cooking pot selection.

A short while later Gwyneth and I were lounging on the sand when the new residents of #1 arrived. Stopping beside the villa, the taxi deposited a middle-aged couple, followed by their thin teenage daughter and a mountain of bags. Soon thereafter, Tristan, in an effort to find his white T-shirt, realized he'd left all his clothes in the drawer at the other villa. Too embarrassed to go fetch them, he sent me. Undeterred by the firmly closed door and the drawn curtains, I arrived on their doorstep, exuding what I hoped was friendliness and a cheerful welcome.

"Hello," I called loudly, rapping on the sliding door.

A man appeared, cautiously opening the door a crack. Joined by his wife and hearing of my mission, they both took on a look of horror at the mention of "boys" being recent tenants in their villa.

"Are you decent, honey?" the father called into the bedroom to his daughter. Good Heavens! I was a female. What did he think was likely to happen if I caught sight of her slightly undressed state? I forget that people can be this modest. And here I was waltzing around in my bikini. No wonder the poor man look so startled. Heading for the bedroom, I found the wife fluttering around me like a brooding hen. Did I look like a thief in beach disguise?

"There they are," I said, pulling open a drawer to reveal all of Tristan's neatly folded clothes. Retrieving them, I hurried out, noticing that both door and curtains were firmly shut behind me. Moments later, we saw the father shaking his daughter's dresser drawers out, presumably to eradicate whatever germs the boys might have left behind. They had looked appalled at the mere thought that we had occupied the villa before them. It was one thing to have some vague notion of previous occupants, but quite another to actually see us in the flesh. Many people would probably cease to use motels altogether if they got a close look at who had occupied the room the night before.

Our next neighborly encounter took place an hour later when the husband approached me on the beach to inquire where Ada had gone. Home, I said, to return at nine the next morning. Consternation crossed his features. Well, they couldn't seem to find a way to lock the place up.

"Oh don't worry," I said. "No one locks up at Out Island resorts. Just take your money and camera with you."

He looked dubious, then rueful. "I guess we're just paranoid, coming from where we do."

Home turned out to be Palm Beach, a place where locking up is second nature. Presumably, paranoia was also the reasoning behind the drawn curtains, the closed door and windows, the inhospitable air. In their absence, no one could see what riches they had left behind, while in their presence, no one could play Peeping Tom. This is what modern, affluent society, the supposed "good life", has reduced us to—suspicious, fearful and reclusive human beings. The wife seemed the most stressed, even to the point of carrying her purse to a deckchair on the beach a few yards from the villa. Taking in the shut and curtained villa, the firmly clutched handbag, the formidable visage, we figured this woman would be a match for any band of thieves.

Approaching us on the beach, she learned what I'd said about not locking up in the Bahamas. Giving me a quelling look, she announced emphatically, "I prefer to lock up."

Next I noticed she was clutching a sheaf of papers which she now began waving under her husband's nose. "It says here that we're supposed to be in villa #2." An angry look was directed at me. I stumbled my way through an explanation that sounded lame at best. It was clear that wifey didn't believe for a second that we'd been moved because of a refrigerator, especially as we were the larger family. Suspicion kindled in her eye, undoubtedly thinking we'd demanded a relocation because of numerous defects in the villa. As Ada wasn't there, however, she had to abandon this line of attack. Frustrated to the core, she ordered a taxi and disappeared on a food shopping spree, returning some hours later with enough food purchases to stop even Tristan and Colin dead in their tracks.

Later, given the mellowing of time in the Bahamas, we learned that the father and daughter were devoted fishermen. They drove the mother wild as she held back meals, waited, fretted, and generally died of boredom while they pursued their passion with a limitless patience. The poor woman was out of her depth, overwhelmed and confused by having given birth to a girl who would rather cast for fish than shop for clothes. Away from her driven presence, father and daughter possessed a serenity, a kind of timeless approach to life that perfectly matched the Bahamian tempo. Watching them in their peaceful pursuit, their unspoken camaraderie, we realized just how ill-formed first impressions can be. Freed of their Palm Beach trappings, their initial discomforts and wifely concerns, they revealed an adaptability as fine-tuned as any veteran traveler's.

* * * *

Travels With Baby:
The Beast of Burden Theory

In Marsh Harbour, Gwyneth discovered a new passion—walking around carrying things. It wasn't enough that she broke our collective backs as we walked her everywhere; now she had to stop, pick up a variety of objects that caught her eye, and lug them with her—the bigger the better, especially such things as large sticks and an assortment of sandals. Having discovered the joys of carrying, she moved on to carrying more than one thing in each hand, a process that involved a lot of dropping and picking up of items. This in turn spawned my Beast of Burden sociological theory. Clearly, Gwyneth is exhibiting man's innate desire to bear burdens, a calling he has been increasingly denying, resulting in a social, emotional, and physical deterioration. If we could all just return to carrying things, and lots of them, ours would be a happier, healthier lot. Gwyneth is living proof.

* * * *

Mermaid Reef

Just off Pelican Shores beach lies a small, man-made feeding reef. Despite its contrived name and artificial origin, a trip there is well worth the short swim, especially in an area like the Abaco Triangle where live reefs are usually less accessible. Easily reached by even young swimmers, it offers excellent viewing of sealife. As the boys said after a trip there, "The good thing about a feeding reef is that the fish aren't scared of you and go hide like those you find on most reefs. So it's easy to see lots of beautiful fish." They loved it.

For a more adventurous snorkeling experience, try a day outing by boat to the reef off Sandy Cay, located south of Elbow Cay. With its extensive coral formations and rich sea life, Jacques Cousteau called it one of the most magnificent reefs in the world. Be prepared for the unexpected, however, as this is no man-made feeding reef. Kevin had the dubious thrill of coming face-to-face with a shark in these seemingly tame waters.

Great Guana Cay

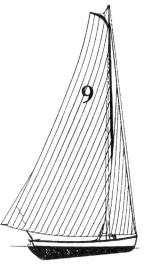

Sparsely populated, scenic, operating a thriving fishing industry, Great Guana Cay possesses a simplicity and authenticity at variance with its Abaco neighbors. The one small village, unpretentious resort and sprinkling of shops, the friendly inhabitants going about their work and almost incidental tourism make it especially pleasurable for those who relish an island tempo. Like a tropical Newfoundland, Great Guana continues its timeless tradition with a refreshing sense of continuity.

The Arrival

Our feeling that Great Guana was different from other Abaco Islands occurred early, about the time we boarded the ferry from Marsh Harbour for the half-hour ride. We could see the island out across the bay, its long, low ridge still covered with undergrowth and trees in contrast to the building boom that has flourished on many other islands. Even the ferry was different, a large craft operated by the Guana Beach Resort rather than one of the prolific "Donnies". In place of the usual clean-cut Man-O-War skipper we found ourselves confronted with Joe, a tall, lanky, friendly type who looked as though he made his living beachcombing. Watching the handful of teenagers clad in their school uniforms (a British tradition that lingers) hop off as the ferry docked, we realized the boat served as school bus in addition to the main source of island and resort transport to and from Marsh Harbour.

The trip was pleasant, offering the usual spectacular waterview of the surrounding island chain. Coming into Great Guana, we were once again curious to see if much had changed over the ten years since our last visit. As the island is less accessible by sailboat because of limited protection in its two anchorages, we had made only brief stops, long enough to observe a general impression of seediness. Then, the resort had been closed, the town somewhat run-down, the island charm slightly tarnished. Man-O-War, in those days, had been more our style, with its tight anchorage, pleasant walks, attractive town, and excellent beach.

We especially wondered about the Guana Beach Resort, a place of mixed repute, now under new management. We recalled the tantalizing vision portrayed by the Visa Card television ad, featuring a dock, beach, and waters we didn't recognize. We had seen the many raised eyebrows we'd produced on neighboring islands when mentioning our projected stay at the resort, a reaction tinged with a mixture of amazement and, we began to suspect, pity. Finally, we had heard of the infamous Guana Grabber, a drink so powerful its mere presence dominated the reputation of the entire resort and was featured in its advertising. Could it be, I suggested to Kevin, that this was not a place for children?

Arriving at the small marina, owned and maintained by the resort, we were led up a path through abundant tropical plantings to our two-bedroom suite, complete with cooking facilities. Access opened out into the central courtyard, with hammocks slung between palm trees, a pool, restaurant, outdoor bar, and a view of the water through the trees. Aside from the rather audible reggae music emanating from the bar area, the place was quiet and convivial, ideal for families as well as couples of all ages. The owners, high-powered New Yorkers in a previous life, had rescued the resort from oblivion, cultivating an enclave of tourism that worked well within the context of this gentle undeveloped island.

* * * *

Island Explorations

Taking Gwyneth for a walk through the village, I noticed it had received a much-needed face-lift since my last visit. A few new homes poked out from among the old; houses I remembered as looking down-at-the-heel now exhibited fresh paint, bright trim, and an air of prosperity in traditional guise. Continuing down "main street" (the only paved street in town), I passed the infamous "fig tree", sporting its habitual handful of drinking enthusiasts. Renowned throughout the Abacos, the fig tree stands strategically beside My Two Sons liquor store, a small enterprise that obviously enjoys a brisk business. One intuitively sensed that the inhabitants of Great Guana and Man-O-War might have their differences.

Up a side road stood a new two-room school, replacing the smaller, wooden one I remembered. Where previously there had only been a couple of pupils, the island now seemed to be enjoying a population surge, judging from the large birthday party taking place in the schoolyard. This is an excellent place for young children to play, with a large grassy area, the usual assortment of playground equipment, a basketball hoop, and hopscotch squares. Beyond and just over the hill lies the outer beach, running the length of the island and generally swept by a sizeable surf. This is one of the most spectacular beaches in the Out Islands, with a nearly endless scope for walking and solitude.

At the far end of town, about a four minute walk from the resort, is the village grocery store, a bit short on goods inside its impressive exterior, but very helpful about ordering anything you might want. Other island enterprises include three gift shops operating out of private homes. A small cafe-restaurant, attached to the grocery store, seemed more oriented to the local populace than soliciting visiting tourists.

As we walked through town, the feeling was of stepping into an island life-style, of gaining a fleeting exposure to what life on a small, sparsely-populated Out Island is really like. Children played along the waterfront, a group of older teens leaped boisterously off the town dock into the water. The sounds of crackling VHF radios could be heard from each house, as owners kept tabs on fishermen and neighbors. A young woman bicycled past, plastic grocery bags dangling from the handlebars and an infant asleep in a Snugli on her front. A new house was under construction, patiently being built by its young owner. One lone golf cart purred past, returning from the grocery store. A handful of island women lingered over coffee and a bit of gossip at the cafe's outdoor table.

Exploring further, I discovered a dirt road heading north, a new raw construction cutting a swathe down-island where once only trees stood in untouched splendor. Later, we learned the road extended three and a half miles, portending a planned two-hundred home development, the kind of menace that continues its relentless assault on the waterfront properties of the world. To a certain extent, the island was opening up. Fortunately, someone was doing some attractive traditional architecture: white wooden clapboard homes with green shutters and gables, very pleasing to the eye, and well integrated into the landscape. One could only hope the trend would continue in the face of development.

Heading south, a paved path led off the main street beside the white church, then turned to dirt, continuing down-island through some of the best walking territory in the Abacos. Tall, dense stands of trees, the sound of singing birds, the beat of the surf on the outer beach, an occasional throb of a passing boat offered almost idyllic surroundings for an island ramble. More than any other Abaco island, Guana has retained its feeling of authenticity, of existing in a timeless way that owes little to the tourist trade. Even the resort has integrated itself well into the community, both through the services it supplies and its unpretentious presence. The passage of years have been kind to Great Guana Cay.

The Guana Grabber & The TV Ad

It doesn't take long at the Guana Beach Resort to discover it's a favorite place with boaters. Arriving daily in droves, they electrify the otherwise somnolent resort each lunch time, congregating at the poolside tables. Despite the reputation for excellent food, it's the Guana Grabber that ultimately draws them, a drink known for

Guana Beach Resort & Marina

Reservations:	800-227-3366 (US)
Direct Phone:	809-367-3590
Direct Fax:	809-367-3590

Location: Just off of the main harbor on the south side of Great Guana Cay.

Accommodations: There are eight beachside double hotel rooms and seven efficiency unit with kitchens.

Getting There: Many airlines service Marsh Harbour airport; take a taxi from the airport to the Conch Inn, then the resort's water taxi to the marina at the Guana Beach Resort.

Local Transport: Walking and bicycling.

Meals: Self-catering as desired in the efficiency units; the resort has a nice restaurant and bar with inside and poolside dining, non-guests welcome.

Amenities: There is a nice little beach at the resort and a beautiful ocean beach a short walk away on the ocean side of the island, a restaurant and pub, small pool, dock, fishing handlines, snorkeling and SCUBA gear, boat rentals, water taxi to and from Marsh Harbour, hammocks, dockage for vessels up to 150 feet at the marina.

Phones: There is a phone at front office and pay phones in town.

Electricity: Utility electricity from Marsh Harbour.

Water: The water at the resort is drinkable.

Laundry: The resort has a laundry service.

Food Stores & Restaurants: Small local food store in the town and the resort restaurant and pub, plus good food stores and restaurants in Marsh Harbour.

Highlights:

• An excellent choice for those who enjoy a casual atmosphere and true island flavor.

• The resort staff is friendly and convivial.

• The peaceful setting is largely untouristed and undisturbed.

• The accommodations are comfortable and some rooms are equipped with kitchens for self-catering.

• The resort offers fine casual dining to guests and day visitors alike.

• Close proximity to the small town and the excellent ocean-side beaches.

• The resort offers daily transport to Marsh Harbour.

its unparalleled potency. Even the welcome sign at the ferry dock proclaims this the "Home of The Guana Grabber". As a result, each day the atmosphere around the pool gradually increases in rowdiness, the decibel level rising in direct proportion to the number of rounds being enjoyed. While many resort restaurants can barely keep their staff busy at lunch, Guana's is hopping. Guana also enjoys the benefit of an excellent central location in the Abacos, within reach of Hope Town, Man-O-War, Marsh Harbour, Treasure Cay and Green Turtle.

The mid-day invasion of thirsty boaters paled in comparison to the impact of having a one-minute Visa Card ad shot on the premises, something the Guana Beach Resort had experienced the previous year. One can only admire the clever, manipulative jockeying of visual aids to create the desirable picture, similar to the screening out of unwanted, peripheral scenery in order to produce the idyllic photograph. Given some rearranging of signs, mixing of beaches, and strategic film splicing, the ad produced a resort location that bore little resemblance to reality. Most amazing, the entire project required no less than two weeks of filming, a crew of hundreds, three barge loads of equipment (brought all the way from Florida), and a presence that threatened to overpower even the soothing effects of the Guana Grabber. Though it's hard to believe, the owner claims all the inconvenience didn't bring him one extra customer. And no—they don't accept American Express.

* * * *

Fishing

Great Guana will always remain the "fishing" island for the boys. Armed with handlines, hooks and conch bait from the resort, they took up a daily stance at the dock, jigging for fish with a success that kept us well supplied with triggerfish and snapper. Local inhabitants, resort employees and visiting boaters all wandered down to offer advice and admire results; one man, arriving in his dinghy off a yacht for lunch, awed them with his technique at catching fish almost as fast as he baited the line. Gwyneth Islay enjoyed the proceedings from the play beach beside the dock, too shallow for swimming, but with nice sand, shade, gentle waves, and even a rope swing for older children. A path, cutting through the dense island growth, led to the rocky point that separated the two harbors, another excellent spot for fishing.

* * * *

Swimming With (Captive) Dolphins

Great Guana Cay can't be mentioned without some reference to the Swimming With Dolphins attraction. Years ago, during our cruising days in the Bahamas, we had spent time anchored off the island's north shore, a lovely, undeveloped stretch with white sand beaches on both sides. It was a tropical paradise, the kind of place boaters eulogize far and wide. As always seems to be the way, some enterprising person with little vision decided such a spot needed "developing". A plan was devised, one that would bring a cruise ship to that very spot, anchoring off the beach and giving the passengers some contrived entertainment on shore, including the much advertised Swimming With Dolphins. Facilities were built, the dolphins penned, and a massive channel dredged, although the only ocean access, through Whale Cay Passage, was known for its rogue waves and often treacherous sea conditions. Given a few seasons, the cruise ship company discovered what any Abaco resident or cruising sailor could have told them—that Whale Cay Passage was largely untenable in winter. The plan was aborted, leaving behind the abandoned facilities, dredged channel, and unfortunate dolphins.

Today, what was once a pristine anchorage now witnesses a daily arrival of tourists to enjoy the expensive and questionable pleasure of swimming with captive dolphins. Needless to say, we didn't go, finding the thought of dolphins in captivity abhorrent and surprising in this day of environmental awareness. Unfortunately, enterprises like this continue to exist, not only because of misguided entrepreneurs, but because pleasure-seeking tourists unwittingly continue to support them. Like so much else in life, it is necessary to see the connection between cause and effect, to realize that one's actions can have a more far-reaching impact than the mere pursuit of pleasure. Wild animals have no place in captivity.

* * * *

Fiddle Performance

Urged on by an enthusiastic Joe, the resort's ferry skipper, Tristan and Colin were talked into a brief fiddle performance in the hotel lobby one night. Joe had first noticed the boys' violin cases when we arrived on the ferry, highly visible pieces of luggage that elicit a range of responses during our travels. There's the periodic eye-brow raiser, the one who can't fathom why anyone, particularly a couple of teenage boys, would chose to travel with violins. Casting a baleful eye at Kevin and me, their sentiments are all too clear—the boys are obviously the victims of overzealous parenting. Then there is the casual response, the mere flicker of the eyelid as it passes over the cases in search of more promising material. Finally, every so often, those violin cases strike a responsive chord, lighting up the passing eye like a light bulb.

"Ah", they sigh with longing, "Do you fiddle?"

Tristan and Colin had done several of these impromptu performances as we traveled the Out Islands, entertaining guests at various resorts as they mingled over their pre-dinner drinks. This time, Joe was insistent, lending Kevin his guitar and stipulating the night. They complied, always willing to play to a receptive audience, drawing guests from their rooms, diners from dinner, the help from the kitchen, and the usual diehard bar crowd. Among the latter were a couple of local island fishermen. Having listened open-mouthed throughout the performance, one of them turned to Joe as if thunderstruck.

"I just came in for a few beers," he said in a bemused voice, "but when I heard that music, I just had to stay." He paused, as if to find the right words before continuing. "It was the most beautiful thing I've ever heard."

No musician could have asked for a better accolade. In retrospect, it encapsulated our island stay, a mixture of island life and quiet resort living, of a responsive people and uncontrived pleasure. For the Abacos, it was a high point.

Green Turtle Cay

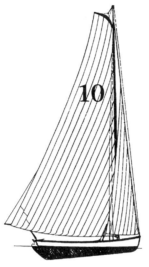

Because of its comparative isolation, Green Turtle seems a world apart, a long way from the well traveled waters of the Abaco Triangle. Uninhabited islands flank it on either side, while the long, wooded shore of Great Abaco stretches to the west, unbroken save for the one small ferry dock. Settled by Harbour Islanders, the village of New Plymouth possesses all the charm and beauty of its predecessor, with narrow, flower-lined streets, small painted New England-style homes, and a show of familiar Abaco names. Self-reliant by necessity, Green Turtle exudes a sense of tradition coupled with modest prosperity. Its pleasures include some lovely outer beaches, pleasant rambles, friendly people, and a charming village.

The Arrival

We were up early to catch the 8 a.m. "school" boat from Great Guana to Marsh Harbour. Getting to Green

Turtle Cay, the next inhabited Abaco Out Island to the north and the last with a village community, included two ferries and a long taxi ride. Despite a separation of only twenty-five miles between the two islands, Whale Cay Passage made the trip by small boat impractical. We'd done the trip by water a number of times ourselves, choosing the right sea conditions and traveling the route in safety and comfort. But without our own boat, the only way to cover the distance was by land and water taxi.

After some friendly negotiations, Kevin secured a taxi ride with Joe Knowles, a congenial Long Islander who'd moved to Marsh Harbour in pursuit of employment. The route to the ferry was familiar, covering much of the same ground we'd traveled on our eventful outing with Peggy Thompson—the same endless expanses of Madeira pine stretching along both sides of the road, the same arrow-straight two lanes, and the occasional Haitian riding a bicycle or waiting patiently for a lift to town. Then we saw the ferry dock, its clearing cut from the tree-lined shore directly opposite the town of New Plymouth. Ferries shuttled back and forth, each leaving as soon as it was filled for the short trip across. Within fifteen minutes after our departure we were entering White Sound, the tight, protected harbor that lies across-island from New Plymouth. Weaving past anchored sailboats, we pulled alongside the Bluff House dock and jumped off. At least, jumped was the intention. Stumbled was more like it, what with our four packs, two violins, one briefcase, assorted straw hats, mats and handbags, and one active baby.

As its name implied, Bluff House was situated on a high point, reached via road or a footpath leading up from the marina dock. We walked, enjoying the shade trees and colorful flowers that lined the path while our luggage was whisked away in a battered VW bus. Past the main building, the tennis courts, and a tantalizing view of the water, we were following another narrower path to our new abode, a bright pink, octagonal treehouse. There we were, literally up in the treetops, with a wonderful living room view out across to Great Abaco and sunlight streaming in through a rustling filter of leaves. Tearing our eyes from the pleasant surroundings, we took stock of the situation. Treehouses, for all their romantic appeal, are not ideally suited to active infants. Hazards beset us on all fronts, throwing the family into immediate action: deck chair across the slider to the suicidal balcony, table and frame packs lashed to the rails of the circular staircase, stool barricade to the kitchen cupboards. By the time we were through, the place was barely recognizable. Gwyneth, however, was content and free to roam. For the moment, at least, the treehouse was home.

* * * *

Going To Town

Getting from White Sound to New Plymouth, the one town on Green Turtle, can be accomplished a number of ways. Where once the trip could be done only by water, covering the five miles that separates the two harbors, a road was recently cut through the island interior, linking the two ends with its raw, barren swathe of gravel and dirt. Easiest and most pleasant for a visitor is to travel by ferry. However, both White Sound resorts also offer some form of free water transport, usually over in the morning and back early afternoon.

By land there's the option of bicycles or walking. Rental cars are out, as there simply isn't anywhere to drive other than to New Plymouth. Bicycling is painless, if dull. We made the mistake of opting to walk.

We finally made it to town after a walk none of us wanted to repeat. Even as a bike ride it would not be ideal—too boring a road, too hot a climate, too little of interest to see. At one point we even found ourselves walking through a new Florida-style development that seemed a sacrilege on Green Turtle, its modern architecture and sculpted landscapes a jarring contrast to the traditional appearance of an Abaco village. Just to show how different tastes can be, however, we later met an American couple who thought the new neighborhood was marvelous, a vast improvement over the quaint, antiquated air of a New Plymouth or Hope Town.

New Plymouth was just as we remembered, with its twisting lanes, tiny streets, and lovely Abaco cottage homes. Here was none of the chic affluence of Harbour Island, the tourist trappings of Hope Town, the dogged modernization of Man-O-War, the simplicity of Guana. Green Turtle seemed to have its own identity, one that gracefully bridged the gap between its nineteen century heritage and the modern age.

We shopped, prowling the three excellent grocery stores, the ice cream shop, the couple of small cafes. A few small restaurants nestled among the homes, ranging from casual to elegant dining. The Albert Lowe Museum, a landmark filled with island lore, graced the main street, housed in one of New Plymouth's oldest and loveliest homes. Up at the school, signs proclaimed the twice-weekly performances of the Gully Roosters, an immensely popular steel band that provides the main source of the island's evening entertainment.

The people were noticeably friendly, eager to chat at the slightest opportunity in the uninhibited way we'd first encountered on the southern islands. Observing our tanned, windblown, slightly scruffy appearance, most assumed we were boaters. We wished we were. No matter how enjoyable the Bahamas are on land, they're even better from a boat.

* * * *

Bluff House Cocktail Hour

Like the Greenwood Inn on Cat Island, Bluff House staged a daily get together of guests before the set dinner hour. Gathered around the glassed-in bar and adjacent pool area, guests congregated to mingle and converse, sampling the tempting array of hors d'oeuvres that graced a central table. The first night Kevin had wandered over unsuspectingly, suddenly finding himself in the midst of a social scene when all he'd meant to do was check out the lobby. Within seconds, Martin, the British manager, had an arm around his shoulders and was snapping an imperious finger at the bartender. A potent fruit punch materialized, hot competition for the Guana Grabber. Cast adrift in the cocktail party atmosphere, he found himself discoursing with a couple from an upscale New England suburb, parents of a teenage son who was clearly bored with the whole low-key Bahamas experience, sullenly waiting for his return home.

Following Kevin's initiation, we all went to cocktail hour, Tristan and Colin quickly becoming part of the permanent throng around the food table while Kevin and I mingled. Following in the wake of an ever-active Gwyneth, I frequently found myself overhearing bits of conversation, the most entertaining a dialogue between

Bluff House Club & Marina, White Sound

Reservations:	809-365-4247
Direct Phone:	809-365-4247
Direct Fax:	809-365-4248

Location: The Bluff house sits high on a hill on the south side of White Sound.

Accommodations: There are rooms with double or twin beds, suites with a bedroom-bathroom upstairs and a lounge downstairs, and villas and treehouses with kitchen facilities.

Getting There: Fly to Treasure Cay International airport, take a taxi from the airport to the ferry terminal, then take a water taxi to the Bluff House.

Local Transport: A water taxi operates to and from New Plymouth, bicycles, and boat rentals.

Meals: Self-catering as desired in the efficiency units; the resort has a nice restaurant and bar with a lively cocktail hour before dinner, non-guests welcome.

Amenities: There is a nice little beach at the resort and a beautiful ocean beach a short walk away on the ocean side of the island, a restaurant and pub, pool, dock, snorkeling, fishing and SCUBA trips arranged, boat rentals, tennis, and gift shop.

Phones: There is a phone at the front office and pay phones in town.

Electricity: Utility electricity from Great Abaco.

Water: The water at the resort is drinkable.

Laundry: The resort has a laundry service.

Food Stores & Restaurants: There are several good local food stores and restaurants in New Plymouth, and the resort has a good restaurant and pub.

Highlights:

• The treehouse villas are especially nice family or group accommodations.

• The Bluff House commands a great view out over the water toward Great Abaco.

• The atmosphere is casual and convivial, especially during pre-dinner hour when guests congregate at the bar for drinks and hors d'oeuvres.

• Dining is excellent, served in the candle-lit diningroom with a complimentary carafe of wine.

• There are frequent ferries and resort transport to New Plymouth Village.

two newly-arrived young couples. The conversation had obviously turned to food, principally what was on the menu that night. As in many other resorts and restaurants in the Bahamas, seafood was a main feature, comprising two out of the three choices for the main course. One of the wives, a petite blonde fluffball had just dropped her conversational bombshell.

"No," I heard her say, "I don't really like any kind of fish." Her tone was timid, almost apologetic.

"What about other seafoods," the young man from the other couple asked. "Do you like them?" Fluffball looked confused, as though unsure what exactly seafood was. "Do you eat shellfish?" he clarified helpfully. "Things like lobster, clams, scallops?"

"Well, I guess so," she spoke hesitantly. "Sometimes...maybe." She paused for a moment, then brightened perceptively, her delicate nose wrinkling for effect. "It's fishy things I don't like."

At seven-thirty the headwaiter appeared, leading the guests into the candlelit dining room where small tables stood invitingly, each graced with a complimentary carafe of wine. Our one meal there came off without a hitch, as Gwyneth was kept occupied in her highchair by a formidable amount of Cherrios, most of which ended up on the floor. The mess seemed a small price to pay for a contented child, particularly considering the advanced hour. By the time the proud cook made his congratulatory rounds among the guests, she'd reached a frenzied stage, reducing us to gulping down apple pie and after-dinner coffee as we made a quick, but satiated, exit.

* * * *

Green Turtle Wet

The next morning we re-encountered "Fluffball" and her husband, this time seated on the front porch of the inn, waiting out a sudden shower. If "fishy" things bothered her, so, quite obviously, did damp ones. By now, her husband looked shrouded in gloom, regarding the inclement weather as the final blow to their shattered holiday plans. In a playful attempt to lighten the atmosphere, I offered up some Green Turtle weather advice, even stooping so low as to imply that the rain was only there because we were visiting. Fluffball looked appalled, only stopping short of asking us when we were leaving.

The truth of the matter is that it has always rained when we were in Green Turtle. Not torrential, raw, sodden rain, but a quicksilver, tropical mist that attacks when least expected, then disappears in a flash of hot sun, only to return again. Frustrating to the newly arrived sunseeker, it always catches us at the end of our Bahamas travels, when hours on the beach no longer seem essential to our enjoyment. We have a number of theories about Green Turtle's wet weather. Perhaps it's the time of year when we visit—the end of April or beginning of May, and the start of the spring rainy season. Or perhaps it's the island's northern location. Certainly the name "green" is applicable, as the island appears lush and brilliant after the parched browns of other Out Islands. The fact that Green Turtle lies in a rain belt seems obvious, given the steady accumulation of clouds on a daily basis. In contrast, Great Guana to the south never seems to get rain. You can sit there in bright sunshine while all around, on Man-O-War, Elbow Cay and Great Abaco, great black clouds are forming.

For us, Green Turtle has always been the Ireland of the Abacos, experiencing a kind of innocuous mist that interferes little with outdoor activities. Beach outings might require a certain amount of preparation for a quick getaway, while island rambles might include the occasional dash for the nearest tree.

* * * *

The Green Turtle Beach Club

Moving day arrived, taking us from one side of White Sound to the other, this time in the most elegant of mini-vans. It hardly seemed to belong in the Bahamas, it was in such mint condition. I opted to walk the short distance with a sleeping Gwyneth on my back, the route a pleasant stroll along a dirt track, first through pine woods, then skirting the harbor shore. Our fanciful treehouse was now replaced by an elegant, poolside room, the kind that can easily accommodate a family of five and still feel empty.

Run with an efficiency the Swiss would admire, the Green Turtle Beach Club presented no unanswered questions, no quests for missing items, or visitor guess-ing games. Female staff members were dressed taste-fully in dark shirts and white skirts, their black hair combed back smoothly into neat topknots. The clientele seemed principally European, with Swiss, German, French and British mingling freely. Presiding over all were Julie, a tall, thin, friendly British woman, and Chris, her soft-spoken Bahamian husband, recent arrivals from the very different world of Nassau. Her children, Julie confided to us, were still in the throes of a readjustment.

Having unpacked and admired the premises, we covered the short distance to the pool, a tempting area with its cushioned lounge chairs, privacy, and small takeout restaurant. A young, attractive family was already ensconced poolside—large athletic husband, pretty blond wife, and two children aged three (Daisy) and nineteen months (Hector), all of them very British. Both children demonstrated an extraordinary aptitude for swimming, Daisy leaping blithely off the edge of the pool while Hector, with waterwings on his arms, delighted in having his father swing him one-two-three over the pool, then let him fly. Each time, Hector, wide mouth split in a huge grin and fat cheeks shining, went flying through the air, disappeared under water, and came up spluttering and gagging. When asked if the children had been enrolled in some waterbabies program, the wife pointed to her husband.

"Just him," she said. "I never watched to see what he did in the beginning. I'd rather not know."

The husband looked pleased with himself. No wonder. We'd never seen anything like it. Hector's durability was further demonstrated later as lunchtime at the pool en famille progressed through soft drinks, hot dogs and ice cream. By now, Julie, her visiting parents, and three-year-old daughter Kelsey had joined the throng. Returning from a trip to our room, I arrived just in time to witness Hector, standing upright in a plastic lawn chair, go pitching over backwards, chair and all, onto the concrete. At the loud crash, Julie let out a cry of concern, both of her parents nearly levitated from their lounge chairs, and Kelsey looked positively riveted. Only Hector's parents remained unperturbed, the mother barely fluttering an eye while the father, casual to the end, rose languidly from his seat, picked up Hector and chair, gave them both a cursory dusting off, and remarked offhandedly, "Don't do that again." Hector, who'd yet to let out a peep, was clearly indestructible.

Green Turtle Club & Marina, White Sound

Reservations:	800-688-4752
Direct Phone:	809-365-4271
Direct Fax:	809-365-4272

Location: The Green Turtle Club is nestled on the waterfront on the north side of White Sound.

Accommodations: The Club's accommodations include 30 poolside rooms and villas, each with a private patio or deck, paddle fans, air conditioning and in-room refrigerator.

Getting There: Fly to Treasure Cay International airport, take a taxi from the airport to the ferry terminal, then take a water taxi to the Green Turtle Club dock.

Local Transport: A water taxi operates to and from New Plymouth, bicycles, boat rentals, and the resort mini-van.

Meals: The Green Turtle Club has fine dining in their indoor dining rooms, breakfast and lunch served on the terrace, and a snack bar by the pool.

Amenities: Beautiful ocean beach on the ocean side of the island; a restaurant and pub; pool, game room, tennis, dock and marina, snorkeling, windsurfing, fishing trips arranged, boat rentals, gift shop, conference room for up to 50 people.

Phones: There is a phone at front office and pay phones in town.

Electricity: Utility electricity from Great Abaco.

Water: The water at the resort is drinkable.

Laundry: The resort has a laundry service.

Food Stores & Restaurants: Several good local food stores and restaurants in New Plymouth, and the resort restaurant and pub.

Highlights:

• The Green Turtle Club & Marina exudes an extra measure of style, polish and elegance.

• As with everything else about the resort, the rooms are tastefully appointed.

• The resort has villas for those who want independence and the ability to self-cater.

• The location is good, beside the harbor yet within easy walking distance of the magnificent outer beach.

• There is a friendly mingling of guests and local residents before dinner for drinks and hors d'oeuvres.

• Dinner is an elegant affair, served in one of three separate, intimate diningrooms with a complimentary carafe of wine.

Capping off the day was a re-encounter with mother and children, this time in the hotel lounge outside the dining room. Clearly frustrated in her desire to eat and socialize with visiting friends, the mother had planted both children in front of the television set with a plate of chocolate cake, a salve that worked only as long as it took an overtired Hector to realize his mother was missing. I arrived from putting Gwyneth to bed to find Kevin plying the mother with the remains of our Bluff House champagne, the previously imperturbable Hector throwing a full-blown fit in his pram, and cake strewn across the carpet. Only Daisy seemed to be enjoying herself, watching the developments with wide-eyed wonder. Taking in the scene, we concluded that for all its glamorous veneer, its international flavor and fashionable air, the Green Turtle Club was, among other things, a place for children.

* * * *

Island Rambles

Aside from the desolate road to town we'd confronted our first afternoon, Green Turtle offers plenty of pleasant walking. Best are the series of dirt tracks radiating out from White Sound, probably sounding a distant death knell to the undeveloped nature of the island. One led to the north tip of the island, through dense, lush tropical vegetation—tall pines, thick bushes, gleaming sea grape, and tiny wild flowers, all of it intensely green. It must have been like this on Elbow and Man-O-War cays before the multitude of houses were built. So far, only a sprinkling dotted the landscape of this end of the island, peeping unobtrusively from the wild landscape. The trouble is that people buy and build, expecting it to always be this way, little realizing that in so doing, they tend to change and destroy what attracted them in the first place. Presently, this ranks as one of the best walks in the Abacos, on a hot day offering plenty of shade, on a wet one, plenty of shelter. Much of it skirts the excellent Ocean Beach, a beautiful long stretch of white sand with little tar, excellent tidal pools for infants, and good swimming. The usual assortment of boat trash lay washed up along the shore, although the Green Turtle Beach Club had done a thorough job of cleaning the portion nearest the resort (after an irate German guest lodged a complaint, proclaiming it a worse offense than the polluted beaches of the Mediterranean).

* * * *

Dining Out

As a final fling, we herded the whole family to dinner at the Beach Club to savor what one resident termed "the best food on the island". Pre-dinner cocktail hour was reminiscent of Bluff House, with hors d'oeuvres, liberally dispensed drinks, and a mingling of guests on the dockside patio. At seven-thirty, Julie led each group to their allotted tables, spread between three small, elegant dining rooms. There again, a courtesy carafe of wine stood in waiting. Obviously a healthy competition was underway, although the atmosphere was quite different between the studied elegance of the Green Turtle Beach Club and the casual flair of Bluff House. Julie wisely led us in first, giving us the table nearest the door so we could execute an unobtrusive exit if necessary. Food arrived promptly: hot fish soup (with lobster and shrimp), fresh bread, and Greek salad. They also provided a lovely wooden highchair for Gwyneth, who proceeded to litter the floor under it with bits of cracker, bread and cherrios. At least in other respects she behaved herself. Devouring everything, we moved on to the main course of grouper served with broccoli and potatoes. Neighbors, we noticed, were an interesting mix: two women traveling alone, a newly-arrived elderly British couple who never spoke two words to each other (the English seem to prefer to dine in silence), and an obvious boat crowd from a charter yacht. Gwyneth reached her tolerance level for highchair entertainment just about the time dessert arrived, a choice of cake, jellyroll or Key Lime pie. Fleeing with the children, I left Kevin lingering over his cup of coffee, a moment of relaxation that was quickly terminated as he caught sight of the approaching waitress. We'd noticed her before, a tall, imposing woman with a haughty expression, aloof manner, and an immense pompadour hairstyle that reflected her imperious air. Pulling back the highchair, she practically recoiled at the sight of Gwyneth's carnage. A look of poison was directed at Kevin as she sniffed disdainfully, then turned and departed without uttering a word. Feeling most uncomfortable, Kevin dived under the highchair, swept up the offending food, and fled.

The next morning, when prowling the hotel premises in search of a cup of coffee, he found himself once again confronted by the daunting waitress. Something approaching a softness flickered across her face.

"You didn't have to clean up under the highchair last night," she remarked. Was this a chink showing in her armor? Sure enough—later the boys were playing by the dining room with Gwyneth when she unbent so far as to coo, smile and wave at the baby. Gwyneth had made another conquest, revealing the kindness under this woman's uninviting demeanor. This is one of the reasons we like traveling with children so much, because it so often brings out the finer side of someone's nature.

* * * *

Colin's Catch

Spurred on by their Guana fishing prowess, Tristan and Colin bought handlines, attached hooks, procured conch bait from the kitchen, and were soon back in business fishing off the marina dock. Colin caught a gray snapper and proudly made arrangements with the chef to have it cooked that night. As we weren't planning to dine in the restaurant, he was dispatched that evening to fetch it from the kitchen. Expecting to receive a small plate of fried fish, he was presented instead by our now favorite waitress with an entire dinner on a tray, complete with fish, side orders of broccoli, peas-n'-rice, loads of bread and butter, and an enormous piece of chocolate cheesecake. That snapper, we later teased Colin, was some catch.

* * * *

An Epic Departure

Even among the annals of Jeffrey family travels, our departure from the Bahamas reigns almost supreme in comic element. The day began with the usual packing up of everything, followed by a walk down our favorite island path one last time. As the weather had deteriorated into more showers than sun, we resorted to some clever rain-dodging along the way. By the time the 12:30 ferry arrived, the rain was a torrent, the kind that only the tropics can deliver. I was lent a voluminous umbrella to get the baby to the boat, but the others (and our gear) had to weather it out as they made the mad dash aboard.

Disembarking on Great Abaco, we caught a five-minute taxi ride to the airport in our snazziest vehicle yet, a sporty, gleaming number that struck pride to the core of its young, street-wise owner ("just bought it this week, man"). Treasure Cay International Airport , as the prominent terminal sign proclaimed it, is the larger of two airports on Great Abaco, located virtually in the middle of nowhere and providing the main transportation link with the outside world. Trotting up to the airline counter in the small one-room terminal, we were greeted with a severe reprimand delivered by a matronly, austere-looking female. Disapproval radiated from her as she perused our tickets.

"Left it kind of late for check-in, didn't you?"

Late? It was one o'clock, the time we'd been told to check in for a 1:45 flight. The flight wasn't at 1:45, she continued. It was scheduled for 1:15. Kevin registered shock. If it was at 1:15, how come when he confirmed it the other day, they said 1:45? She shrugged, indicated all too clearly that we were obviously trying to wheedle our way out of this one. Kevin's emotions were up, however, and he wasn't going to buckle under to any misplaced blame. "What man works here?" he demanded. "I confirmed my flight with a man."

"No man works here," she smirked, obviously feeling she'd scored one this time.

"Well, I talked to a man and he confirmed our flight and what time it left."

"Where'd you call?" she asked.

"Right here," he said, indicating the number on the airline information brochure. She looked, smirked more than ever, then threw in a hefty snort for good measure.

"You called that number?" she laughed.

"Of course I did. It says Abaco, and this is Abaco, so that's the number I called."

Such logic was clearly sheer idiocy to her. "That ain't this airport. That's Marsh Harbour. They don't know nothin' about flights here. You're supposed to call Ft. Lauderdale," she added, as though addressing a particularly dense child. "You ain't confirmed here, so you might not get on that plane." At the rate this conversation was progressing, it seemed to me the plane must have long since taken off. In the meantime, Kevin was telling her to get on the phone and call Marsh Harbour. It was at this point that she delivered her pièce de resistance. "Ain't no phone here." We should have known, Treasure Cay International Airport had no phone. In fact, there was no way of communicating with Marsh Harbour airport, a mere twenty miles away, other than by driving there in person. As one airline official put it, "the only way we know a flight has arrived is when the pilot walks through the door."

Pressed for more information, the woman at the counter revealed that the plane was a nine-seater with six passengers already booked, plus goodness knows how many others coming on in Marsh Harbour. As our family required four seats, we were clearly in trouble. She finally admitted we might be four of the original six.

"But there may be more comin'," she added irrepressibly.

Due to the bad weather, we soon discovered that few flights were arriving or departing, a situation that rendered the lack of communication all the more compelling. Over the ensuing hours of waiting we discovered only one other couple on our flight, elderly Floridians off their sailboat from Treasure Cay. In the meantime, I was at leisure to watch the various airline employees fill the hours with a formidable capacity for cheerful chitchat, something Bahamians specialize in. No matter what, they always seem to have something to say to each other, usually punctuated with plenty of laughter.

As the hours passed, a boring affair in the loud, stark, concrete terminal building, our partners in flight grew restless. Finally taking matters into his own hands, the husband called a friend in Florida from his cellular phone, who in turn called the airline office in Ft. Lauderdale, then relayed the message back that yes, a flight would be arriving about 4:30. By now, this whole situation was beginning to resemble a spoof of an international airport—something dreamed up for a TV comedy. We had the restless passengers, the helpless desk clerks, the mysterious flight arrivals (yes—various commercial planes were still arriving now and then), the complete lack of communication with the other airport a few miles down the road (not to mention the rest of the world). Gwyneth was doing her best to pick up every piece of trash in the place and eat it, while the boys had reached a near-catatonic state. Even the weather was acting up. You had the feeling that when five o'clock rolled around, all the employees packed up and went home, oblivious to the state of affairs left behind. We had plenty of time to observe other passengers—departing visitors with straw hats in tow, disgruntled looking arrivals, horror struck at the damp weather, and one lone boy, whiling away the time by devouring a steady supply of chips, soda, candy, and culminating in an entire pack of gum as he boarded his plane.

At four-thirty our plane finally arrived, driven by a pilot whose entertaining presence almost made up for the delay. Piling in with alacrity, we flew to Marsh Harbour, the pilot demonstrating his impressive, signature landing of gliding engineless right up to the terminal door. The rest of the flight was uneventful and smooth, despite the unsettled weather, with the plane flying above one set of clouds and below the other.

Our arrival four hours late was executed with unaccustomed civility. Escorted by the solicitous pilot, we collected luggage, then headed for customs, the only potential sticky point in our three months of travel. While the rest of us all had our passports at the ready, Gwyneth was traveling in a free-spirited fashion, without a scrap of official identification to her name. We'd simply forgotten the whole issue of her recent arrival until we'd landed in the Bahamas, a country that takes its bureaucracy with a grain of salt. American customs officials are a different breed—they regard each new arrival on U.S. turf with the suspicion of a finely-tuned guard dog.

While the pilot hovered nearby, the unsmiling customs official received our four passports, flicked them open, cast identifying glances at each of our faces, then came to a screeching halt at the sight of Gwyneth Islay.

"So," he said, drawing the word out with ominous precision, "this is the baby with no passport, is it?" A pause of studied length followed while we waited expectantly. Something indefinable flickered across his face. "Well," he continued at last, looking across the counter at Gwyneth's fascinated stare. "I think we'll have to hold her for questioning."

After two glorious months in the Bahama Out Islands, we were home free.

*　*　*　*

Avalon House Publishing

Adventuring with Children `NEW`

An Inspirational Guide to World Travel and the Outdoors
by Nan Jeffrey

Now in its third edition, this book shows families how to combine low-budget worldwide travel with challenging outdoor activities.

"Sure to become a classic of family adventure traveling."
—*Backpacker* Magazine

"Makes camping with kids actually sound fun. Much more sophisticated than most child-oriented vacation guides."
—*New York Daily News*

"Such a practical guide — and such a joyful celebration! that most families will find it a very valuable addition to their library."
—*Home Education Magazine*

$14.95 • ISBN 0-9627562-4-5 • Soft • 325 pages • 8-1/2" x 11" • 50 Photos • Avalon House Publishing

Best Places to Go

A Family Destination Guide to the World
by Nan Jeffrey
This is a travel book everyone can enjoy. It provides just the right combination of information, inspiration and insight into 22 of the world's best travel destinations in Eastern North America, Central America, The Caribbean, and Europe. This book provides all the essential details active travelers need to plan their itinerary with confidence.
$14.95 • ISBN 0-935701-75-3 • Soft • 350 pages • 5-1/2" x 8-1/2" • Illustrations • Avalon House Publishing

The Complete Buyer's Guide to the Best Outdoor & Recreation Equipment

by Kevin Jeffrey
This consumer guide truly lives up to its billing as the most comprehensive, up-to-date equipment planning resource for active travelers. It reviews the huge assortment of trip-related outdoor gear currently on the market, helping the buyer make the best choice. Saves readers money and time.
$14.95 • ISBN 0-935701-90-X • Soft • 450 pages • 5-1/2" x 8-1/2" • Illustrations • Avalon House Publishing

Bahamas — Out Island Odyssey `NEW`

by Nan Jeffrey

An inspirational, entertaining guide to one of the world's best travel destinations, written by the world's premier family adventure writer, Nan Jeffrey. It offers insight gained from her family's two month trip through the scenic, peaceful Bahama Out Islands, Long, Cat, Exuma, Eluethera, Harbour Island, Elbow Cay, Man-O-War Cay, Great Abaco, Great Guana, and Green Turtle. As with all her books, the message to adventuring families is "You can do it!"

$14.95 • ISBN 0-9627562-3-7 • Soft • 256 pages • 8-1/2" x 11" • Photos • Avalon House Publishing

Sailor's Multihull Guide to the World of Catamarans & Trimarans

by Kevin Jeffrey and Charles Kanter
A one-source guide to the world of cruising multihull sailboats, featuring detailed information on chartering, buying or building, owning and outfitting, and sailing and handling. With this unique reference book you'll be able to review and compare 150 of the world's best cruising catamarans and trimarans, including current production boats, past-production models on the used boat market, stock designs for custom building, and commercial craft. Each boat is presented in a large two-page format, complete with illustrations and specifications.
$24.95 • ISBN 0-9627562-1-0 • Soft • 464 pages • 7-1/4" x 9-1/4" • Illustrations • Avalon House Publishing

800-247-9437